Thought: A Very Short Introduction

VERY SHORT INTRODUCTIONS are for anyone wanting a stimulating and accessible way in to a new subject. They are written by experts, and have been published in more than 25 languages worldwide.

The series began in 1995, and now represents a wide variety of topics in history, philosophy, religion, science, and the humanities. The VSI Library now contains more than 300 volumes—a Very Short Introduction to everything from ancient Egypt and Indian philosophy to conceptual art and cosmology—and will continue to grow in a variety of disciplines.

Very Short Introductions available now:

Available soon:

For more information visit our website
www.oup.com/vsi/

Tim Bayne

THOUGHT

A Very Short Introduction

OXFORD
UNIVERSITY PRESS

Great Clarendon Street, Oxford, OX2 6DP,
United Kingdom

Oxford University Press is a department of the University of Oxford.
It furthers the University's objective of excellence in research, scholarship,
and education by publishing worldwide. Oxford is a registered trade mark of
Oxford University Press in the UK and in certain other countries

First Edition published in 2013

Impression: 1

British Library Cataloguing in Publication Data

Data available

ISBN 978-0-19-960172-1

Printed in Great Britain by
Ashford Colour Press Ltd, Gosport, Hampshire

*This book is dedicated to my parents,
who taught me how to think.*

Contents

Acknowledgements

I would like to thank Peter Carruthers, Michelle Montague, Jennifer Nagel, Christoph Reisinger, and especially Jakob Hohwy for their comments on various chapters.

List of illustrations

Chapter 1
What is thought?

> Man is but a reed, the most feeble thing in nature; but he is
> a thinking reed.
>
> Blaise Pascal

What is thought? This might seem like a strange question to pose
at the outset of a book, for it is a fairly safe bet that anyone bold
enough to read a book—especially a book on thought!—will not be
unaccustomed to thinking. In fact, you have probably already had
quite a number of thoughts today. Although there may be periods
during the course of a normal day during which one has few
thoughts—perhaps there are even times at which one's mind is
completely free of thought—a life devoid of thought would not be
recognizably human. Whether the thoughts in question are banal
('I'm hungry'), alarming ('He's got a gun!'), profound ('Some
infinities are bigger than others'), or downright bizarre ('I am the
left foot of God'), there is no denying that thinking comes
naturally to human beings. We might say that thought is to human
beings what flight is to eagles and swimming is to dolphins.

But it is one thing to think and quite another to understand
the nature of thought. Just as eagles fly without any grasp of the
principles of aerodynamics and dolphins swim without
understanding the physics of flotation, so too most of us think
without having any real insight into the nature of thought.

Thinking may be commonplace, but it takes a rather peculiar bent of mind to think about thought itself.

The study of thought straddles a number of disciplines. Philosophers explore the logical structure of thought and the relationship between thoughts and other mental phenomena, such as perceptual states and bodily sensations. Psychologists study the processes that underpin our capacity to think and the ways in which these processes can be disrupted. Neuroscientists probe the neural machinery of thought, and anthropologists investigate cultural variation in modes of thought. Linguists examine the relationship between thought and language, cognitive ethologists study thought in non-human species, and researchers working in computer science and artificial intelligence explore ways in which thought might be realized in non-biological systems. In this book I draw freely on these disciplines to provide an introduction to some of the many fascinating aspects of thought. Of necessity, the coverage provided here will be highly selective; some aspects of thought will be mentioned only in passing, and many others will be entirely overlooked. But the ground that we do cover will, I hope, whet your appetite for further investigation into what is surely one of the most fascinating topics there is.

Thinking clearly about a topic often requires making distinctions, and thinking clearly about thought is no exception to this general rule. The term 'thought' can refer to three quite different features of mental life. Firstly, 'thought' can refer to a certain kind of mental *faculty*. Just as there are mental faculties associated with the capacity to see and to hear, so too there is a mental faculty—or perhaps faculties—associated with the capacity to think. The faculty of thought raises a number of questions. What does the possession of such a faculty require? Which creatures have such a faculty? What is the relationship between the faculty of thought and other mental faculties, such as those involved in perception and language?

Secondly, 'thought' can refer to a certain type of mental *state* or *event*. To think of an object is to have it before one's mind in some way. Of course, there are ways of bringing an object 'before one's mind' that do not involve thought. For example, seeing an object involves bringing it before one's mind, but although we can—and often do—think about the objects that we see, seeing something is not as such a way of thinking about it. Although it is not easy to say exactly what is involved in bringing something before one's mind in the way that is distinctive of thought, the phenomenon is familiar enough. When Tolstoy says of Anna Karenina, 'And so only by occupation in the day and by morphine at night could she stifle the fearful thought of what would be if he ceased to love her,' we immediately recognize her state of mind. But can we go beyond a merely intuitive grasp of thoughts and attain an understanding of their nature? Can we say how thoughts differ from other kinds of mental events, such as bodily sensations, perceptual experiences, or emotional states? Can we identify the ways in which one kind of thought (e.g. realizing that one's bill has been incorrectly calculated) might differ from another (e.g. wondering whether the coffee is ready)? And what is the fundamental nature of thoughts? Can they be explained in terms of physical states of some kind, or must we appeal to some kind of non-physical reality in order to account for them?

A third feature of mental life to which the term 'thought' is applied concerns a distinctive kind of *activity*. Just as one can be occupied by the task of looking for someone or listening to something, so too one can be occupied by the task of thinking about something. We excuse ourselves by saying that we were 'lost in thought'; we decline to discuss a topic with the confession that we are 'too tired to think about it'. We describe some people as 'deep thinkers' and others as 'slow thinkers'. Indeed, intellectuals are sometimes described simply as 'thinkers', as if they have a monopoly on this kind of activity! Here too the nature of thought poses many questions for us. What exactly is involved in actively thinking about a topic? Are there different types of thought processes? If so, how are they related to each other? What norms should guide the activity of thinking?

We will not be able to answer all of the questions that have just been raised, but we will be able to make a start on them. Let us begin with the faculty of thought.

The faculty of thought

The French philosopher René Descartes once described thought as a 'universal instrument which can be used in all kinds of situations'. What might he have meant by this statement?

Consider the contrast between perceiving an apple and merely thinking about it. In order to perceive an apple there must be a direct causal connection between the apple and you. The light that illuminates the apple must be reflected by it and then processed by your visual system. By contrast, no such direct causal connection is required in order to think about an apple. Perception requires direct contact with the objects of one's awareness, but thought does not. Further, in order to perceive an object certain kinds of quite precise environmental conditions must obtain. In order to see an apple fall from a tree the tree must be within one's line of sight; in order to hear an apple land on the ground its falling must occur within earshot. Technology enables us to overcome these limitations to some degree—mirrors allow us to see objects that are behind us and microphones allow us to hear events that occur in remote locations—but even when such factors have been taken into account perception is still dependent on the environment in a way that thought is not. One can think about an object even when it is shrouded in mist or hidden in a soundproof room. We can capture these points by saying that whereas perception involves a form of 'engaged' and 'stimulus-dependent' contact with the world, thought allows a creature to represent its environment in a 'disengaged' and 'stimulus-independent' manner. In other words, whereas the perceptual faculties can be used only in certain kinds of situations (when the object is present and when the environment cooperates), the faculty of thought can be used 'in all kinds of situations', as Descartes put it.

The fact that thought represents objects in a 'disengaged' and 'stimulus-independent' manner allows us to think about objects in their absence. We can think about events that have not yet occurred and we can think about events that will never occur; indeed, we can think about events that could never occur. This capacity allows us to anticipate the consequences of certain events in advance of their happening and to prepare for them. If the anticipated consequences of an event are positive then one might attempt to bring it about; and if those consequences are negative then one can take steps to prevent it from occurring. Thus, a creature with the capacity for thought can control its environment in a way that a creature that is reliant only on perception cannot.

A second feature of thought that Descartes's description points us to concerns its *scope*. Whereas perception provides us with access to only a small range of things, the reach of thought is (practically) unlimited. The range of things that a creature can perceive is constrained by the features of its perceptual faculties. We cannot see objects that are very small, we cannot hear sounds that are very high in pitch, and we cannot detect odours that are very faint. But there is no such limit on the range of objects that we can think about. We can think about objects that are far removed from us in both space and time. Indeed, we can think about things that are imperceptible in principle, such as numbers or subatomic particles. As long as one has some way of locking on to an object one is able to think about it. All one needs is a name ('Genghis Khan'; 'Burkino Faso') or a description ('The barista at the cafe on the corner'; 'the greatest Brazilian footballer') and one can think about a thing.

A particularly important respect in which the range of thought is unrestricted concerns the kinds of properties that it allows us to detect. Again, the contrast with perception is instructive. It is possible to see that an apple is red or that it has an indentation on one side, but only a creature with the power of thought is able to appreciate the fact that the apple originated in Western Asia, or that the apple has more genes than the human genome. In other words, thought enables us to grasp features of the world that are not perceptually accessible to us. A creature that possesses only perceptual capacities can respond to the physical features of its environment, but it cannot respond to its economic, political, or psychological features. It cannot take steps to nullify the effects of inflation, participate in an election, or attempt to convince someone that their views are mistaken. (Is thought's capacity to represent the world *absolutely* unbounded? Probably not—thought too may have its limits as we will see in the final chapter. But it is likely that there are relatively few limits on the scope of thought.)

A third feature of thought that Descartes's description points us to is its systematic, integrative, and open-ended nature. Thought allows an individual to relate one state of affairs to another—to grasp the connections between events that lie beneath the appearances of things. Consider a famous episode in the history of medicine involving the Hungarian physician Ignaz Semmelweis. Whilst working at a hospital in Vienna, Semmelweis noticed that the incidence of puerperal (childbed) fever was much higher in one ward than it was in another. Semmelweis also noticed that the medical students who worked in the ward with the higher rate of infection had just performed autopsies whereas those who worked in the other ward had not, and he wondered whether the students might be infecting the pregnant women with 'cadaverous material'. He tested this hypothesis by requiring the medical students to wash their hands with calcium hypochlorite—a substance that was known to remove the smell associated with performing autopsies—before attending the pregnant women. Instituting this practice led to a dramatic drop in the death rate from puerperal fever. Semmelweis's research—which laid the foundations for the germ theory of disease—required two acts of thought: not only did he need to grasp the hitherto unnoticed connection between the activities of the medical students and the contrasting rates of puerperal fever, he also needed a way of testing his hypothesis.

This episode in the history of science provides a striking example of the integrative and creative power of thought, but we make use of these powers on a daily basis. Whether one is trying to plan an overseas vacation on a limited budget, attempting to juggle a hectic work schedule with challenges posed by raising children, or just trying to figure out the best way to get from A to B, most of us spend much of our lives thinking about the relationship between events. Indeed, the integrative powers of thought are revealed not only in theoretical and practical reasoning but also in humour. Getting a joke typically requires appreciating connections between topics that are normally unrelated. (There are two fish in a tank. One says to the other, 'How do you drive this thing?')

An important aspect of the systematicity of thought is that the capacity to have certain types of thoughts is intimately bound up with the capacity to have other types of thoughts. A creature that is able to entertain the thought that Marco is taller than Valentina ought also to be able to entertain the thought that Valentina is taller than Marco (and vice versa). This capacity is explained by the fact that thoughts are compositional. Thinking that Marco is taller than Valentina requires that one have a way of thinking about Marco, a way of thinking about Valentina, and a way of thinking about the 'taller than' relation. But if a creature is able to think about Marco, Valentina, and the 'taller than' relation, then it is able to think both that Marco is taller than Valentina and that Valentina is taller than Marco. The systematicity of thought is a very important feature of it, for it is what makes rationality possible. A creature that possesses the relevant concepts can infer that if Marco is taller than Valentina and if Valentina is in turn taller than Ilia then Marco must also be taller than Ilia, thus adding to its stock of knowledge.

We have seen that Descartes's description of thought as a 'universal instrument which can be used in all kinds of situations' captures three central features of thought. Firstly, it captures the fact that thought involves the capacity to represent objects in a stimulus-independent and environmentally disengaged manner. Secondly, thought involves capacity to represent a (relatively) unbounded range of objects and properties. Thirdly, thought involves the capacity to represent one's environment in a structured and open-ended manner, a capacity that underpins the potential for rationality and insight.

Before we move on, we should recognize that the conception of thought that has just been sketched is an idealization, and that a creature's capacity to represent the world might measure up to this idealization in some respects but fall short of it in others. For example, some creatures may be able to represent objects in their absence, but be able to represent only a very restricted range of their properties. Alternatively, there may be creatures that can represent various domains in thought-like ways, but have relatively limited abilities to think about the possible relations between those domains. What should we say about such cases?

I think we should say that a creature possesses a faculty of thought *to the extent that* it is able to represent the world in the ways outlined above. There may be no clear and bright line that separates those creatures that can think from those that cannot. Instead, we should recognize that there may be creatures—young children and non-human animals, for example—whose representational powers fall well short of the 'ideal specifications' for thought but which are thought-like to some interesting degree. Indeed, even creatures (such as ourselves) who clearly and unambiguously qualify as thinkers might fall short of these specifications in certain ways, for we do not always put two and two together.

Types of thoughts

Let us now turn our attention from thought as a faculty to thought considered as a distinctive kind of mental event or state. What distinguishes thoughts from other kinds of mental events and states, and what distinguishes thoughts of one kind from thoughts of another kind?

Suppose that you are at a bonfire. You can see the sparks emitted by the fire and you can hear the roar of the flames. These are of course perceptual events of various kinds, but you may also find yourself thinking about the bonfire. You might find yourself wondering how exactly combustion works, or wondering about what would happen to the bonfire if the wind suddenly changed direction. These thoughts will be prompted by your perceptual experience, but they are not themselves forms of perception. We can also contrast thoughts with bodily sensations. It is one thing for the bonfire to make one uncomfortably hot, but it is quite another to merely consider the possibility that the bonfire might make one uncomfortably hot. More generally, we need to distinguish sensing one's body from thinking about one's body. A local anaesthetic might prevent one from having sensations in one's foot, but it would not prevent one from being able to think about one's foot.

Although thoughts are distinct from perceptions and bodily sensations, there are many important points of contact between thoughts on the one hand and perceptual states and bodily sensations on the other. For one thing, perceptual states and bodily sensations can trigger certain thoughts. Hearing noises in the street might cause one to jump to the conclusion that a fight has broken out between one's neighbours; odd sensations in one's chest might lead one to wonder whether one is having a heart attack. Sensory states do not merely cause one to have thoughts of various kinds, they can also provide evidence for those thoughts. One might justify the thought that the neighbours are fighting by drawing attention to the noises in the street; similarly, one might defend the hypothesis that one is having a heart attack by referring to the odd sensations that one feels in one's chest.

Although the distinction between thoughts on the one hand and sensory states (such as perceptions and bodily sensations) on the other hand is not difficult to grasp at an intuitive level, providing a clear and rigorous articulation of it is far from straightforward. Some theorists claim that thoughts can be distinguished from perceptual states and bodily sensations in virtue of the fact that thoughts involve the deployment of concepts whereas sensory states do not. The idea here is that although one can visually identify an object as a cat without possessing the concept of a cat, one cannot think about a cat without possessing the concept of a cat. However, the attempt to distinguish thoughts from sensory states in this way is controversial, not merely because many theorists claim that perception does involve concepts but also because it has proven very difficult to say precisely what concepts are.

Other theorists suggest that thoughts can be distinguished from sensory states by appeal to the notion of conscious character—'what it's like' to be in a certain kind of mental state. Some theorists claim that thoughts—unlike sensory states—do not have any conscious character at all. According to this position, whereas there is something distinctive that it is like to see a rainbow or hear a piano being played, there is nothing distinctive that it is like to think about a rainbow or a piano. Other theorists claim that there *is* something distinctive that it is like to have a thought, but that what it's like to have a thought is very different from what it is like to enjoy a perceptual state or a bodily sensation: whereas sensory states have a purely 'sensory character', the experiential character of thoughts—it is alleged—is distinctively cognitive. (Yet a third group of theorists finds talk of the conscious character of thought very obscure, and is not at all sure that they know what precisely this debate is about!) Certainly there is no consensus about whether thoughts can be distinguished from sensory states by appeal to the notion of conscious character. (What do you think? Does it seem like there is something distinctive 'that it is like' to have a conscious thought?) In sum, although we seem to have a pretty robust capacity to distinguish thoughts from perceptual and sensory events, there is no settled account of precisely what this distinction amounts to.

Let us turn now to the question of how thoughts of one kind differ from those of another. There are two dimensions along which thoughts can be distinguished from each other. The first dimension concerns what the thoughts are *about*. We can think about particular entities—such as Senegal, Julius Caesar, or the number 6. We can think about classes of things, such as the class of people who own exotic animals or the class of individuals who have walked on the moon. We can think about properties, such as being six foot tall or being older than one's siblings. We can think about states of affairs, such as the fact that the cat is on the mat, or the fact that the dog is not on the mat. We can think about possibility and necessity—about *the way things could have been but are not* or *the way things are and must be*. We can think about things that do not exist, such as Zeus or Sherlock Holmes.

There are two ways of referring to the things that a thought is about: we can refer to such entities as the *objects* of thought, and we can refer to such entities as the *contents* of thought. ('Content' here is short for 'propositional content'.) Each of these ways of talking is useful, and we will avail ourselves of both of them.

The second dimension along which thoughts differ concerns the *attitude* that the thinker takes to the objects or contents of thought. Consider thoughts about the availability of coffee at breakfast. One person might *believe* that there is coffee at breakfast, another might *desire* that there is coffee at breakfast, and a third might *intend* that there be coffee at breakfast. Each of these terms—'believe', 'desire', 'intend'—pick out different attitudes that one can take to the same state of affairs. (Some authors use the term 'mode' instead of 'attitude' here.)

Taken together, these two dimensions provide us with what we might call the *propositional attitude* conception of thought. However, although this conception of thought is illuminating, we would be unwise to *identify* thoughts with propositional attitude states. We can see why by reflecting on the nature of belief. Ask yourself the following question: 'On what continent are the Andes to be found?' Now that you have put this question to yourself, you are—I presume—thinking about the Andes. But now consider the mental state that you were in five minutes ago, when you had not yet considered this question. Although you were not thinking about the Andes, you did (I presume) believe that the Andes are in South America. (If someone had said of you then that you believe that the Andes are in South America, what they said would have been true.) What this suggests is that one can believe that something is the case even when one is not thinking about the matter in question. We can refer to such non-occurrent states as dispositional beliefs. In fact, the vast majority of our beliefs are merely dispositional, for we only ever consider a fraction of our beliefs at any one point in time. What goes for belief applies also to other kinds of propositional attitude states, such as desire and intention. One can desire to run a marathon or intend to get married without actually thinking about either of these topics at the time in question.

How does this bear on the relationship between thoughts and propositional attitudes? The connection is this: although propositional attitude states can be dispositional, thoughts themselves cannot be dispositional. To say that someone is thinking about the Andes is to commit oneself to the claim that they are in an occurrent, and presumably conscious, mental state that is about the Andes in some way. By contrast, to say that someone has Andes-related beliefs, desires, or intentions is not to commit oneself to any such claim. We might say that the word 'thought' is reserved for the occurrent manifestations of propositional attitudes.

The exercise of thought

Thus far we have considered thought as a particular kind of mental faculty and as a particular kind of mental state or event. Let us turn now to a third aspect of thought: thought as a mental activity. In other words, let us consider *thinking*.

In order to understand thinking we need to understand the ways in which thoughts are related to each other. Although thoughts can occur in isolation—while waiting at a traffic light one might suddenly be struck by the thought that friendship is a fundamental good—it is perhaps more common for thoughts to occur as components of trains of thought, sequences of thoughts that are related to each other in some way.

There are two ways in which the components of a train of thought can be related to each other. Some trains of thoughts involve only *associative* relations. As the Scottish philosopher David Hume observed, 'thoughts introduce each other with a certain degree of method and regularity'. Hume went on to identify a number of relations of association by means of which thoughts 'introduce' each other, such as the fact that the objects of one thought might resemble those of another. To use Hume's own example, sometimes the thought of a picture leads one to think of the object depicted in the picture. Associative thinking is familiar from daydreams and other forms of reverie. One begins by wondering whether films that are based on books are in general as good as the books on which they are based, which leads one to wonder what films have recently been released, which in turn causes one to wonder what day of the week it is, which reminds one of a deadline, and so on.

Trains of thought that are linked by associated relations can be contrasted with trains of thought that are linked by *inferential* relations. Consider the thoughts 'Socrates is a human', 'All humans are mortal' and 'Socrates is mortal'. The components of this train of thought are inferentially connected, for if the first two thoughts are true then the third thought must also be true. To take another example, consider the thoughts: 'The mail is generally delivered by 9 a.m.', 'It's now 9:30 a.m.', 'The mail has been delivered'. This train of thought also involves inferential relations, for the first two thoughts provide one with reasons to endorse the third thought. These two inferential trains of thought can be contrasted with associative trains of thought, in which (say) a thought about a graveyard might elicit a thought about one's mortality, or a newspaper story about the possibility of a postal strike might cause one to consider whether today's mail has already been delivered.

The contrast between associative trains of thought and inferential trains of thought is of crucial importance in many contexts. Consider two strategies that a prosecuting lawyer might employ in order to gain a conviction. One strategy is that of attempting to elicit in the minds of the jurors a train of thought which takes the jurors from thoughts about certain facts regarding the case (the location of the body; the fingerprints at the scene) to the thought that the accused is guilty by means of logical and evidential relations. Another—and rather more disreputable—method that the lawyer might employ is that of encouraging the jurors to have trains of thought which associate the accused with the crime. For example, the lawyer might point out that the accused resembles a notorious criminal in appearance, thus causing the jurors to have thoughts that will naturally 'introduce' the thought that the accused is guilty.

Although there is a delight to be had in following a purely associative train of thought, the power of thinking resides in the fact that it enables us to track the logical and evidential relations between thoughts. Indeed, we tend to reserve the term 'thinking'

14

for the activity of keeping track of such relations. It is the ability to grasp the inferential relations between thoughts that enables detectives to solve crimes, allows scientists to test hypotheses, and provides fans of Sudoku with the ability to complete their puzzles. Much of the value of thought derives from our ability to organize our thoughts into coherent trains so as to 'see' what follows from what. In other words, much of our interest in thinking concerns *reasoning*.

Psychological research suggests that reasoning can take two forms. Some reasoning is automatic and intuitive whereas other reasoning is controlled and reflective. (This distinction is often referred to as a distinction between 'System 1' reasoning and 'System 2' reasoning.) Automatic reasoning is quick and mostly unconscious, whereas controlled reasoning is slow and generally under conscious control. The distinction between automatic and controlled reasoning is not a hard and fast one but marks out two ends of a continuum, and many instances of reasoning fall somewhere between the 'purely automatic' and the 'purely controlled'.

The contrast between these two modes of reasoning is most clearly revealed by cognitive illusions, contexts in which our intuitive and spontaneous judgements are at odds with those that are considered and reflective. One of the most extensively studied cognitive illusions involves a task that was developed by the psychologist Peter Wason in the 1960s and is now known as the Wason selection task. Suppose that you are presented with four cards (see Figure 1), and are told that every card has a number on one side and a letter on the other side. You are then asked to check whether the cards conform to the following rule:

Rule: If a card has an S on one side, then it has a 3 on the other side.
Question: Given that every card has a letter on one side and a number on the other side, which card (or cards) *must* you turn over in order to determine whether the rule is broken?

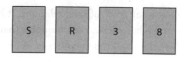

1. The Wason selection task

My guess is that you are intuitively inclined to think that you need to turn over only the first and third cards. Is that response right? Well, you do indeed need to turn over the first card, for if it does not have a 3 on it then the rule is wrong. Do you need to turn over the second card? No, for it does not matter whether the number on the other side is 3 or not. But you do not need to turn over the third card either, for the rule could be right whether or not this card has an S on its other side. (It does not matter if this card has (say) an R on the other side, for the rule says only that if a card has an S on one side then it has a 3 on the other side.) However, you *do* need to turn over the fourth card, for if it has an S on the other side then the rule is false.

The Wason selection task is evidence of a gap between intuitive thought and reflective thought, for by thinking the problem through one can come to see that one's intuitive response is incorrect. Surprisingly, the temptation to endorse one's intuitive response to the problem seems to persist even after one has consciously reflected on it. Just as the lines of the Müller–Lyer illusion look like they differ in length even when one knows that this is not the case, so too it is tempting to think that one needs to turn over only the first and third cards even when one knows better.

We share the capacity for automatic and intuitive reasoning with many other species, but controlled and reflective reasoning appears to be a distinctively human trait. As such, we have some—albeit perhaps, rather limited—capacity to shape and sculpt it. We can stand back and consider not just how we *do* think but how we *should* think. We are not restricted to the modes of thought that come with our evolutionary and social inheritance, but—by thinking about thought—we have the ability to develop new and better ways of thinking.

Where should we look for principles that might govern the evaluation and regulation of thought? Many theorists have suggested that we should look to the formal systems of logic and probability theory here. But although logic and probability theory provide us with some pointers as to how we ought to think, their usefulness in this regard is surprisingly limited. For one thing, at best logic and probability theory tell one what one should not think rather than what one should think. Here is why. Suppose that you believe that all ducks can swim and you also believe that Donald is a duck. If all ducks swim and Donald is a duck then it must be the case that Donald can swim, but does that mean that you should *believe* that Donald can swim? Not necessarily, for someone might have presented you with good evidence that Donald cannot swim. So what should you do? Perhaps you should give up the belief that all ducks swim. Or perhaps you should give up the belief that Donald is a duck. (Donald might look like a duck, but not everything that looks like a duck is a duck.) Or perhaps you should wonder whether the evidence for thinking that Donald cannot swim was as good as it appeared to be. Logic alone does not indicate what one should do, and any one of these responses might be appropriate, depending on the details of the case. The only thing that logic tells you is that 'All ducks can swim,' 'Donald is a duck,' and 'Donald cannot swim' cannot all be true.

A second limitation of logic and probability theory is that neither discipline takes into account the constraints under which we must think. Thinking is always situated in a particular context, and what counts as good thinking depends on the constraints that govern the relevant context. One set of constraints derives from the features of one's environment. In some contexts one has all the time in the world to think through a problem, and the need to get the right answer is more important than getting a speedy answer. (Consider an engineer who needs to determine how deep the

17

foundations for a building must be.) In other contexts time is of the essence, and a rough approximation to the truth that is arrived at quickly might be better than a perfectly correct verdict which arrives too late to be of any use. (Consider a pilot who is attempting to discern the cause of engine trouble.)

Another set of constraints on what counts as good thinking derives from features of the agent's own mind. Agents differ in their cognitive capacities, and what counts as good thinking will depend on the contours of those capacities. An exercise of thought that is remarkable in a six-year-old might be completely routine when carried out by an adult, for example. A good example of the need to keep these considerations in mind concerns the oft-made claim that one should not have inconsistent beliefs. On the face of things, this prohibition would seem to be unproblematic given that inconsistent claims cannot both be true. But in order to comply with this injunction a creature must have some way of searching through its store of beliefs so as to check for inconsistency between them, and for creatures like ourselves who have hugely complex belief structures and limited processing capacities this is a hugely daunting task.

So, any account of the norms of thought must take into account both the features of the agent's environment and their own cognitive capacities. At best, logic and probability theory deal with 'unbounded rationality'—the kind of rationality available to creatures with unlimited time and computational power. But we are required to reason under conditions of temporal pressure and with limited powers of computation. Any viable set of what Descartes called 'rules for the direction of the mind' should draw on the formal structures explored by logic and probability theory, but it must also take into account our capacities as finite creatures. In other words, any adequate account of how we *should* think must be informed by an account of how we *can* think.

Chapter 2
The mechanical mind

The brain has muscles for thinking as the legs have muscles
for walking.

La Mettrie, *Man the Machine*

What does it take to be a thinker? It has sometimes been argued
that thought requires a certain kind of non-physical medium—a
soul or an immaterial mind. Although this is perhaps the
common-sense view of thought, it has few contemporary advocates
in science or philosophy. Most contemporary theorists endorse a
physicalist account of thought, according to which thinking is a
capacity that purely material creatures can possess. Whether or
not we ourselves are purely physical creatures, there is nothing in
our nature as thinkers that indicates otherwise.

There are three general motivations for physicalism. The first
motivation concerns its ability to account for the correlations that
obtain between states of the brain and states of thought. Whether
they involve the relatively mild changes that are consequent on
ingesting caffeine or the rather more radical changes that result
from stroke and other forms of brain damage, we know that the
state of the brain is intimately correlated with our capacity to
think. By exploiting such correlations, scientists are beginning to
acquire the capacity to detect a person's thoughts by measuring
their brain states, as we shall see in the next chapter. The simplest

explanation for such correlations is that thoughts are identical to, or at least realized by, states of the brain.

A second motivation for physicalism concerns its capacity to account for the causal role of thoughts. Thoughts are both caused by physical events and in turn function as a cause of physical events. The pattern of light hitting one's retina might lead one to believe that someone has walked into the room, and this belief might lead one to extend one's hand in greeting. A conception of thoughts as physical states offers the hope of accommodating the causal role of thoughts, whereas it is less clear how causal interaction between thoughts and physical events would be possible if thoughts are realized in a non-physical medium.

A third reason to endorse physicalism is that it does justice to the continuity of nature. We know that creatures capable of thought evolved from purely physical creatures that lacked such a capacity. Although one cannot rule out the possibility that this process involved the emergence of some kind of non-physical medium, it is surely more plausible to assume that the evolution of thinking creatures can be explained by appeal to changes in the structure of purely physical systems, in much the way that the evolution of living creatures can be explained by appeal to changes in the structure of non-living systems.

So, we have three good reasons for endorsing the physicalist view of thought. None of these reasons is individually decisive, but taken together they provide a strong case for taking the physicalistic conception of thought very seriously.

The computational theory of thought

It is one thing to have reasons for the view that thought *must* be a purely physical phenomenon, and quite another to have an account of how thought *could* be a purely physical phenomenon. Although it takes many forms, there is only one account of how thought could be realized in a purely physical system. This account does business under various labels—'the representational theory of the mind', 'the computer model of the mind', 'the symbol systems hypothesis'—but I will refer to it as the *computational theory of thought* (CTT).

In order to present CTT we must first introduce some terminology. Let us begin with the notion of a formal (or 'syntactic') property. A formal property is a property that a symbol has in virtue of its form. It is a property that a purely physical system can be sensitive to. Some of the most familiar formal properties are shape properties. Consider the various ways in which one might write the word 'monkey':

monkey   MONKEY   *Monkey*

These three tokens of the word 'monkey' differ in important respects, yet each is a recognizable instance of that English symbol. It is in virtue of the shapes of these three words that they each count as instances of the English word 'monkey.' Written language employs shape properties, spoken language employs acoustic properties, and signed language employs movement properties, but there are no principled limitations on the kinds of physical properties that can function as formal properties. One could have a representational system in which electrical charge, temperature, or weight functioned as formal properties, distinguishing symbols of one kind from symbols of another.

The formal properties of a symbol can be contrasted with its *semantic* (or contentful) properties, where these concern the thing (object, property, relation) that the symbol refers to or means. (The story is actually a bit more complicated than this, for we need to allow that symbols can have different semantic properties even when they refer to the same object, but that complication need not concern us here.) In English, the symbols 'monkey' and 'bananas' have the content <monkeys> and

<bananas> respectively, for those are the objects that these two symbols refer to. Note that two symbols can have different formal properties but the same content. For example, the English word 'monkey' and French word 'singe' both refer to monkeys, but they do not have the same formal properties, for they have different 'shapes'.

So much for terminology; what does CTT actually say? We can think of CTT as comprised of two claims: a claim about the nature of *thoughts* and a claim about the nature of *thinking*. In a nutshell, CTT holds that thoughts are sentences in a 'language of thought', and it claims that thinking involves formally governed transitions between sentences in a language of thought. Let us unpack these two ideas in detail.

What does it mean to say that thoughts are sentences in a language of thought? Consider the thought that Marcel has a monkey. Just as the sentence 'Marcel has a monkey' is built up out of linguistic symbols that have particular contents—for example, the word 'Marcel' refers to Marcel and 'monkey' refers to monkeys—the advocate of the language of thought claims that the thought that Marcel has a monkey is also built up out of symbols that have particular contents. Thinking that Marcel has a monkey involves tokening mental symbols that refer to Marcel, monkeys and the having relation in such a way that, taken together, these symbols form a structured representation with the content <Marcel has a monkey>.

The phrase 'the language of thought' might suggest that the advocates of this position are committed to the idea that the compositional structure of thought must be modelled on that of language. However, although one of the most influential advocates of the language of thought hypothesis, the American philosopher Jerry Fodor, does indeed claim that the compositional structure of thought is indeed language-like, one could endorse CTT without being committed to that view. Instead, one could think that the structure of thought has more in common with that of maps or diagrams and is not particularly language-like. In other words, the advocate of CTT might suggest that reference to the 'language' of thought should be taken with a large grain of salt. What CTT *does* require is that thought has a compositional structure, such that the parts of a thought make independent contributions to its meaning.

The ideas just sketched constitute the heart of the computational theory of thought, but there is one more element that must be mentioned before we turn to the question of thinking. As we noted in the previous chapter, thoughts have *attitudes* (or modes) in addition to contents. Asher might *believe* that Marcel has a monkey; Luka might *intend* that Marcel have a monkey; and Nat might merely *hope* that Marcel has a monkey. So, CTT will need an account of what it is for a particular symbol structure to be a belief as opposed to an intention or a hope. The most popular solutions to this problem hold that the attitudinal component of a thought is a matter of its functional role—the ways in which it combines with other symbol structures to guide the agent's behaviour. The kinds of behaviours associated with the belief that Marcel has a monkey differ from those associated with intending that Marcel have a monkey or merely hoping that he has a monkey, and what it is for Marcel's thought to be a belief (rather than a hope or an intention) is for him to be disposed to engage in those behaviours rather than any others.

Let us turn to the account of thinking provided by CTT. What does it mean to say that thinking involves formally governed transitions between sentences in a language of thought? Suppose that I have the thoughts 'All men are mortal' and 'Frank is a man', and that these two thoughts lead me to form the thought 'Frank is mortal'. CTT explains this transition in thought by appealing to the formal properties of the symbols (or, better, complexes of symbols) that are involved in it. If we had a mechanism that was sensitive to these properties, then it might take us from the first two thoughts to the third thought without knowing anything about what these thoughts mean (that is, their semantics). The idea is that the machinery of thought operates in much the same way as the Post Office's automated address reader functions. Although the reader does not know anything about Mr Smith or Ms Jones, it is able to ensure that their mail gets to them because it is sensitive to the formal (or syntactic) differences between 'Smith' and 'Jones'. As the philosopher John Haugeland memorably put it, 'If you take care of the syntax, the semantics will take care of itself.'

That, in essence, is the computational theory of thought. In a nutshell, the idea is that thoughts are symbol structures, and thinking involves the manipulation of these structures on the basis of their formal properties. Of course, it is not clear that thinking feels like symbol manipulation, but CTT does not make any claims about what it feels like to think. (As we noted in the previous chapter, there is little agreement about what, if anything, it does feel like to think.) Rather, CTT is an account of how purely physical creatures could be thinkers.

Inside the Chinese room

Although CTT is an influential view, it is not without its detractors. Indeed, criticism of the idea that thought can be explained in purely mechanical terms dates back to the 17th-century philosopher Gottfried Leibniz, who argued that 'a sentient or thinking being is not a mechanical thing like a watch or a mill: one cannot conceive of sizes and shapes and motions combining mechanically to produce something which thinks'.

Leibniz's intellectual heir in this respect is the philosopher John Searle, whose 'Chinese room' objection to CTT has been influential. Searle asks you to suppose that you are located in a room into which Chinese messages are sent. (For the purposes of the thought experiment, Searle assumes that you do not understand Chinese, and thus that the messages are meaningless to you. Readers who do understand Chinese might want to amend the story in the appropriate manner.) Although you do not understand the messages, you have access to a giant 'look-up' table that maps each of the messages that you receive to a suitable response. For example, if you receive the Chinese version of the question 'What do monkeys eat?' the look-up table might direct you to produce the Chinese equivalent of 'bananas', or some other sensible reply.

Searle claims that although someone in the Chinese room would be able to manipulate symbols in the appropriate manner, they would not be thinking. What this shows, Searle says, is that mere symbol manipulation does not suffice for thought—genuine thought requires something more. But since CTT equates thought with symbol manipulation it must be false. (Searle's own account of what thinking involves is somewhat elusive and need not detain us here.)

Broadly speaking, we can sort the various responses that have been made to Searle's Chinese room objection into two camps. Some responses take issue with Searle's assumption that there would be no thought in the Chinese room, whereas others allow that although the Chinese room might be devoid of thought, there are important disanalogies between the Chinese room scenario on the one hand and the conception of thought represented by CTT on the other, such that one could endorse CTT without being committed to the claim that thinking can occur in the Chinese room. Let us consider these two responses in turn.

Is there any reason to endorse Searle's assumption that no genuine thought occurs in the Chinese room—that there is only symbol manipulation? A critic might argue that the intuition that the Chinese room scenario is devoid of thought arises because we focus on the wrong aspects of the scenario. We naturally imagine ourselves in the position of the person in the Chinese room manipulating squiggles without any comprehension of what they mean. But, says Searle's opponent, CTT is not committed to the idea that there is a 'homunculus' (that is, a 'little person') who understands the meaning of the symbols that it manipulates. Rather, the idea at the heart of CTT is that symbols are manipulated purely on the basis of their formal properties—the whole *point* of the account is that they *do not* have to be understood in order to be manipulated. (CTT could hardly claim to have provided an explanation of thinking if it turned out that one needed to think in order to manipulate symbols in the language of thought.) The appropriate analogue of the thinker is not the person in the Chinese room but the Chinese room *as a whole*, and for all we have seen thus far there is no reason to deny that the system as a whole can think. (For this reason, this response is often called the 'systems reply'.)

The system's reply can be further motivated by considering whether the person in the Chinese room—or rather, the Chinese room as a whole, to be more precise—could pass what is known as the Turing test. The Turing test was proposed by Alan Turing, who suggested that it should be regarded as a sufficient condition on the possession of thought. (Turing did not that it should also be regarded as a necessary condition on thought.) In essence, the Turing test runs as follows. Suppose that there are two rooms, one of which contains a normal human being and one of which contains the 'target'—an entity whose status as a thinker is in question. Both rooms are linked by a communication channel to an interrogator, who has the job of identifying which room contains the human and which contains the target. The interrogator is allowed to put questions of any kind to the two individuals, and the target can be said to have passed the Turing test if, after an extended session of questioning, the interrogator is unable to determine which room the target is in.

Would someone in the Chinese room be able to pass the Turing test? Perhaps not—at least, not if passing the test requires one to produce one's answers to the interrogator's questions under 'real-time conditions'. For one thing, the computational demands on using a look-up table to conduct a typical conversation are enormous, and it might not be possible to engineer a Chinese room scenario that could keep pace with a normal human being. But if we waive the demands of real-time responses then there does not seem to be any reason to deny that someone in the Chinese room could pass the Turing test—after all, that is precisely what the look-up table is designed to ensure.

But should we regard passing the Turing test as validation of an entity's claim to be a thinker? I think not. In fact, many theorists have argued that the Turing test is too weak and that something else is required for true thought. We can explain what that something else might be by considering an important disanalogy between the structure of the Chinese room and the account of thought provided by CTT.

A central feature of the Chinese room scenario is its appeal to a look-up table. Because of this fact, there is no substantive structure in the way that the system generates the output that it does. Suppose that the person in the Chinese room (let's call him Max) is presented with the following two questions (written in Chinese): 'What animal is often used as a beast of burden?' and 'What animal is descended from the African wild ass?' Max will answer both questions by consulting his look-up table, and find that in both cases he is directed to the Chinese word for 'donkey'. But what this process fails to take into account is the fact that these two sentences have a concept in common—the concept <donkey>. But one of the things that thought requires is that one grasp the distinctive contribution that each of a thought's constituent concepts makes to it. In order to truly grasp the thoughts 'The donkey is used as a beast of burden' and 'The donkey is descended from the African wild ass' one must appreciate that the two thoughts have a common subject matter—namely the donkey.

But no appreciation of this fact—or indeed, of any fact like it—is present in the Chinese room. Neither Max nor the system in which he is embedded need represent—even implicitly—that the two thoughts mentioned above are both about monkeys. In other words, the look-up table operates along entirely non-compositional lines. Genuine thought, by contrast, *is* compositional. This fact is accommodated by CTT, for various 'sentences' in the language of thought will have elements in common. It is in virtue of this fact that genuine thinkers are able to comprehend sentences that they have not previously encountered, such as 'Monkeys rarely ride unicycles.' By contrast, a creature that is reliant on a look-up table to generate its behaviour will be restricted to the information contained in that table, and will fail to make sense of novel input.

Of course, we could modify the Chinese room scenario so that Max's responses are informed by the fact that 'Monkeys like bananas' and 'Monkeys live in trees' have a common constituent, namely the concept <monkey>. But now that we have made this modification it is no longer so clear that genuine thought and understanding are absent from the Chinese room. (Again, we need not assume that Max understands what the symbols mean—rather, understanding might be present only in the system as a whole.) We have built into the Chinese room dispositions that go some way towards capturing the fact that thought is a 'universal instrument which can be used in all situations'.

Grounding the contents of thought

Another important challenge to CTT concerns the task of explaining how the symbols of the language of thought acquire their content. In virtue of what is the meaning of a thought grounded? What makes it the case that the mental symbol for <monkey> refers to monkeys rather than to (say) meringues, mopeds, or marsupials?

One proposal appeals to features of natural languages. Suppose that a person's medium of thought is simply their native language. So, if Polish happens to be your mother tongue, then Polish would also function as your medium of thought. According to this version of CTT, the symbols in the language of thought would acquire their contents in much the way that the symbols of natural languages—that is, certain sounds, marks on paper, and movements—do. And how do natural language symbols acquire their content? By means of conventions. For example, English employs the convention that 'monkeys' refers to monkeys. Of course, there is no convention that a particular brain state refers to monkeys in the way that 'monkey' does. Rather, the idea is that thought takes the form of inner speech (or inner writing and inner signing), and the mechanisms of thought can appropriate the conventions which govern the particular language that one is speaking (writing, signing).

But this solution to the problem of grounding content has relatively few adherents. Although many theorists allow that certain *kinds* of thought involve the internalization of natural language, it is widely held that—for the most part at least—the symbols which constitute the language of thought are not drawn from natural languages. On this view, we do not think in Chinese or Portuguese but in 'Mentalese'. There are two main motivations for this view. Firstly, as we will see in Chapter 4, there is evidence that non-linguistic creatures are capable of certain kinds of thought. If that is so, then one's language of thought cannot be equated with one's natural language. A second reason for the view that the language of thought cannot be a natural language is that thinking of a kind is required to learn the conventions that govern natural languages. Neither of these two lines of argument is uncontroversial, but together they have persuaded many theorists that even if much distinctively human thought may be encoded in natural language, there must also be a more primitive 'language of thought' that is independent of one's natural language. And if that is right, then the symbols in the language of thought cannot acquire their contents via convention in the way that the symbols of natural languages do. But if mental content is not based on conventions, what is it based on?

Someone might be tempted to suggest that mental content does not depend on anything, and that the meaning of a mental symbol is one of its primitive or brute properties. This proposal might solve (or perhaps 'dissolve') the grounding problem, but unfortunately there is little else to recommend it. In the same way that the English word 'monkey' is no more naturally associated with monkeys than with any other type of object, it is difficult to see why the brain state that functions as the symbol for monkey in the language of thought should be associated with monkeys as opposed to any other type of object. Instead, the only plausible account of how it is that a mental symbol acquires its content requires that we appeal to the relational features of brain states. But what kind of relational features could ground a thought's content?

Historically, many theorists have suggested that resemblance might play a role in explaining how mental symbols acquire their contents. This idea was essentially the account that the British Empiricists (such as John Locke and David Hume) gave of how the mind represents the world. Symbols in the language of thought—'ideas', in the terminology employed by the Empiricists—mean what they do because of what they resemble. In a nutshell, the idea of a monkey refers to monkeys because it resembles monkeys.

There are, however, serious problems with this account. For one thing, resemblance is ubiquitous, and any brain state resembles multiple objects. Some of my brain states will resemble some of your brain states, but surely it does not follow that my brain states represent your brain states. In order to have any plausibility the advocate of this account must identify the kind of resemblance relations that underwrite mental content, and that has proven very difficult to do. A second problem is that we can think about all manner of things that do not resemble brain states in any way. In what sense could the mental symbols for <beauty>, <truth>, and <justice> possibly resemble the properties of beauty, truth, and justice? Thirdly, and perhaps most fundamentally, it is not at all clear how mere resemblance might explain why a mental symbol has the meaning that it does. Even if a brain state does happen to resemble (in some relevant sense) a certain feature of the world, it is utterly mysterious why this fact should entail that it represents that feature of the world.

A rather more promising solution to the content-grounding problem appeals to causal relations. Roughly speaking, the idea is that a mental symbol means (or refers to) the object or property that activates it. If a symbol functions as a monkey detector then it means monkeys. In a slogan, a particular symbol means <monkey> if it is 'set up to be set off' by monkeys.

Although this account is rather more plausible than the resemblance account, it is not without problems. Some of those problems are ones that it shares with the resemblance account. For example, it too struggles to explain how we are able to think about abstract properties, such as beauty, truth, and justice. The advocate of the causal account will need to explain how we are able to enter into causal relations with these properties, and it is far from obvious that any such account can be given. A similar challenge is posed by thoughts about non-existent objects, such as Zeus or Sherlock Holmes, for non-existent objects do not enter into causal relations. (Indeed, a version of this problem is posed by thoughts about objects that will—but do not yet—exist, such as tomorrow's newspaper.) The causal theorist will need to ground our capacity to think about objects with which we have had no causal interaction in a more primitive level of thoughts about objects with which we have interacted. Some such account might be viable, but it is not yet clear precisely how the story will go.

The causal account also faces problems when it comes to objects that we have interacted with. One such problem is generated by the possibility of *misrepresentation*. We must allow for the possibility that one could mistake (say) a bear for a monkey. But if that is right, then the causal theory of content is in danger of entailing that the monkey symbol means something like <monkey-or-bear-that-resembles-a-monkey> rather than <monkey>, for the symbol in question is 'set up to be set off' by both monkeys and bears that look like monkeys. (Remember: on the proposal under consideration, a symbol's meaning just is whatever it is that causes it to be activated, and this symbol will be activated by both monkeys and bears that look like monkeys.) But that is not the result that we want. Instead, we want to be able to say that one *mistakes* the cleverly disguised bear for a monkey. This is known as the *disjunction problem*, for the problem is that the causal theory entails that the <monkey> symbol means <monkey-or-X> for any X that is reliably mistaken for a monkey. It is beyond the remit of this chapter to consider the various solutions to the disjunction problem that have been offered, or indeed any of the solutions to the other problems that confront the causal account of content. Instead, I must leave you to explore these fascinating issues on your own. Suffice it to say that providing a plausible account of how the symbols in the language of thought acquire their meaning remains an ongoing challenge.

My aim in this chapter has been to introduce the computational theory of thought, and to explore—albeit only briefly—a couple of the leading challenges to it. We have not, however, said much about what the alternatives to it might be. Let us bring this chapter to a close by asking whether there might be other ways in which thought could be realized in a purely physical system.

Although the computational account represents the dominant account of how thought might be realized in a physical system, a number of influential voices have questioned whether the structure of thought itself must be mirrored by the neurofunctional processes that underpin it. Perhaps, some have suggested, the systematicity of thought emerges from neurofunctional processes that are fundamentally unstructured. The philosopher Ludwig Wittgenstein captured the spirit of this proposal when he asked: 'Why should the *system* continue further in the direction of the centre? Why should this order not proceed, so to speak, out of chaos?'

Something of the spirit of Wittgenstein's remark animates contemporary accounts of thought that appeal to dynamical systems theory and certain types of connectionist networks. Such views are physicalist in that they have no role for a non-physical medium of thought, but they depart from CTT insofar as they reject the assumption that there must be some form of isomorphism between the neural processes responsible for thought and the structure of the thoughts that these processes generate. In Wittgenstein's terms, they conceive of the order of thought as proceeding out of 'neuronal chaos'. Although these views are endorsed by only a minority of theorists, they do represent an important challenge to the computational theory of thought, and the dust has not yet settled on the question of whether they might provide a viable alternative to the conception of thought on which we have focused here.

Chapter 3
The inner sanctum

Like the notes of an old violin,
Thoughts talk to me within
My mind, that shuttered room.

Siegfried Sassoon, 'Old Music', in
Rhymed Ruminations

In Greek mythology the god Momus is said to have expressed
dissatisfaction with man because his state of mind could not be
easily discerned. Instead, Momus suggested, human beings ought
to have been built with a window in their breast so that their
mental states could be more easily identified. The idea that a
person's thoughts might be hidden in the secret recesses of their
mind is not an unfamiliar one. Uncertainty about another's
mental life is perhaps most often triggered by an encounter with a
non-human animal or someone from a culture that is radically
different from one's own, but it can also be elicited by contact with
those with whom one is most intimate. When waking in the early
hours of the morning, one might wonder what is going through
the mind of the person lying next to one.

Thinking, then, seems to be a private activity. Thoughts seem to be
actors in a private theatre—a theatre with room for an audience of
only one. No one else has—or *could* have—the kind of immediate

and direct access to your thoughts that you enjoy. You can, of course, communicate your thoughts to someone else if you so choose, but you can also 'keep your thoughts to yourself', as one says. Unlike the movements of one's body which are in principle (if not always in practice) 'open to view', the contents of one's mind are private, limned by the boundaries of one's own awareness.

This conception of thought is often described as Cartesian, for we owe much of its influence to the work of René Descartes. In this chapter we will focus on the epistemological elements of the Cartesian picture—its account of our access to thought. There are two theses to consider here. The first thesis is that first-person thought is *transparent*: one's own thoughts are directly or immediately accessible to one. The second thesis is that third-person thought is *opaque*: the thoughts of other people are not directly or immediately accessible to us, but are available only indirectly. Indeed, we shall see that the Cartesian view threatens to undermine the assumption that we can have any kind of access to the thoughts of others.

Both components of the Cartesian account have been subjected to intense criticism over the last century or so. Some theorists reject the thesis that our own thoughts are transparent to us; others deny that the thoughts of others are opaque to us; and still others reject both of these theses. This chapter will introduce you to some of the most influential criticisms of the Cartesian picture, and will consider what might remain of it once those criticisms have been taken into account.

A mind of one's own

In what sense might one's own thoughts be transparent? There is little reason to think that the *nature* of our thoughts is transparent to us. Some people take thoughts to be brain states, others take thoughts to be functional states that are realized by brain states, and still others take thoughts to be states of an immaterial soul.

Scientific investigation and philosophical analysis are required to adjudicate between these proposals, and it is clear that introspection provides one with little insight into the ultimate nature of one's thoughts.

It is also clear that the *origins* of our thoughts are not typically transparent to us. We often have little idea about what the causes of our thoughts might be, or why we are drawn to have one thought rather than another. Consider the following question: 'Which country is bigger, Canada or Brazil?' Although you may be strongly disposed to provide one answer rather than another, you are not likely to know the factors that underlie this disposition. Even when we do have beliefs about the provenance of our thoughts there is no reason to think that such beliefs enjoy any special kind of authority. Other people are often better placed to explain the genesis of our thoughts than we ourselves are.

But despite all this, it is hard to resist the thought that there is *something* to the transparency thesis. Consider two people, Meg and Nathanael, who are playing the guess-a-number game. Meg thinks of a number between 1 and 20 and Nathanael attempts to guess what that number is. Suppose that Nathanael guesses that Meg is thinking of 14, but Meg denies that he has guessed correctly. Nathanael does not have to take Meg's denial at face value—he might, for example, suspect Meg of fibbing—but it would be very odd for Nathanael to accuse Meg of having made a *mistake* about what number she was thinking of. If Meg takes herself to have been thinking of 14 then—we assume—she must indeed have been thinking of 14.

The point generalizes to any thought that occurs within the stream of consciousness. When it comes to the question of identifying these items, there does not seem to be anything that one needs to do. One's conscious thoughts seem to be immediately given to one. One is simply aware that one is (say) thinking about what to have for lunch, or wondering whether one's flight will be delayed, or realizing that one has locked one's keys in the car. The suggestion that one could misidentify one's thoughts—that they might be other than they 'appear' to be—is hard to take seriously. It is in this sense—and perhaps this sense alone—that the Cartesian commitment to the transparency of first-person thought has some plausibility. (Is this kind of transparency restricted to one's own thoughts, or could someone equipped with 'brain-reading' technology have this kind of access to someone else's thoughts? We will consider this question below.)

It is important to recognize that the scope of transparency that we have just identified is restricted to conscious thoughts—thoughts that occur within the stream of consciousness. It is clear that we do not have direct and immediate access to the identity of our standing propositional attitudes—our dispositional beliefs, desires, and intentions. Suppose that you are asked who Ronald Reagan's first wife was. You might know the answer to this question in the sense of being able to produce an answer to it in most ordinary contexts, but you might not be able to recall the answer if you are tired, have recently suffered concussion, or are inebriated.

Indeed, we can even be *wrong* about the identity of our standing propositional attitudes. Mechanisms of self-deception might blind us to the nature of our own beliefs, desires, and intentions. A person might explicitly reject racism—they might genuinely take themselves to be free of racist attitudes—but close inspection of their behaviour might reveal patterns in it that are best explained by supposing that they have racist attitudes. In fact, a significant branch of social psychology is concerned with investigating the degree to which such 'implicit' attitudes govern our everyday interactions. But because these attitudes are unconscious we have no transparent access to them, and there is no reason for the Cartesian—or anyone else for that matter—to think that we will be reliable in self-ascribing them.

The minds of others

The version of first-person transparency that we have just presented is rather more modest than many versions of the thesis that have been defended, but it is nonetheless strong enough to generate a striking contrast between the first-person case and the third-person case. As we noted at the start of the chapter, we are often deeply uncertain about what conscious thoughts, if any, might be passing through someone else's mind. Indeed, given the Cartesian conception of thought as actors on an inner stage, the challenge is not that of explaining the errors that we make in tracking the thoughts of others but of explaining why we are so *good* at tracking the thoughts of others. So, how *do* we tell what other people are thinking?

Psychologists are still in the process of figuring out the answer to this question. Although the details are not all in, it is clear that we use a variety of cues to 'read' other people's mental states. Some kinds of mental states—particularly emotional states—are perceptible in behaviour. We can see joy written on a person's face and in the way that they move; we can hear fear and uncertainty in their voice. Other kinds of mental states are less closely tied to particular patterns of behaviour, but can nonetheless be identified with some reliability on the basis of behavioural cues. In many contexts, people think about the objects that form the focus of their perceptual attention; thus, one can often tell what someone is thinking about by identifying what it is that they are looking at or listening to (for example). But for linguistic creatures such as ourselves the most important clues about another person's state of mind are provided by what they say—or, as the case may be, what they *do not* say. Even taking the possibility of deception and miscommunication into account, it is a reasonable bet that if someone says that the kitchen is on fire then they believe that the kitchen is on fire.

In introducing the Cartesian conception of thoughts as actors on an inner stage, I suggested that this view threatens to undermine the assumption that we can have any kind of access to the thoughts of others. How exactly does that threat arise? After all, it is one thing to say that there is an asymmetry in the kind of access that we have to our own thoughts and that which we have to the thoughts of other people, but it is quite another thing to suggest that we lack any kind of reliable access to the thoughts of others. Why might the Cartesian conception of thought generate the radical sceptical worry that the minds of others are *never* accessible to us?

Consider the following thought experiment developed by Ludwig Wittgenstein in his *Philosophical Investigations*, involving a society in which everyone has a box in which they keep a beetle. Each person can examine their own beetle, but no one has access to anyone else's beetle—one has access only to the boxes in which the beetles are kept. Wittgenstein points out that although the beetles in our respective boxes might be identical, we would not have any evidence for that view. After all, you have never seen the beetle in my box, and I have never seen the beetle in your box. We might know that the boxes in which we keep our beetles are identical, but we would not—it seems—have any reason to think that the beetles themselves are identical.

What does this have to do with our access to the thoughts of others? Well, suppose that you say 'The kitchen is on fire.' Although I might take your utterance to express the same thought that I would express were I to say 'The kitchen is on fire,' it is not clear that the Cartesian is able to justify this assumption, for on the Cartesian account there is no 'internal' or 'intrinsic' connection between the identity of a thought and its behavioural manifestation. Just as boxes of the same kind can house beetles of different kinds and beetles of the same kind can be housed in boxes of different kinds, so too the Cartesian must allow that the same forms of behaviour can result from thoughts of different kinds and thoughts of the same kind can lead to different forms of behaviour. But if that is so, then how can we be justified—as we clearly are!—in ascribing a mental state to someone on the basis of their behaviour? This is the heart of the infamous 'problem of other minds'.

Wittgenstein's aim in presenting the beetle-in-the-box analogy was not to argue that there really is a problem of other minds but to demonstrate the bankruptcy of the Cartesian view by showing that it undermines our capacity to ascribe thoughts to each other. Given that we clearly *can* identify each other's mental states with some reliability, any account of the nature of thought that implies that such a capacity is unobtainable must itself be wrong. Of course, someone who is deeply committed to the Cartesian view will not be moved by Wittgenstein's line of argument—the Cartesian might insist that the assumption that we do have access to the thoughts of others is precisely what is up for grabs—but Wittgenstein's argument will give pause to anyone not deeply in the thrall of the Cartesian picture.

Why exactly does the Cartesian account generate the problem of other minds? The problem arises because the Cartesian views the relationship between a thought and its behavioural manifestations as contingent. Just as there is no necessary connection between a beetle and its box, so too there is no necessary connection between a thought and the behaviour to which it gives rise. So, one way to defuse the problem of other minds—indeed, perhaps the only way to defuse it—would be to embrace a conception of thought on which the connections between a thought and its behavioural manifestations are internal or non-contingent. What might such a view look like?

The doctrine of behaviourism provides one conception of thought according to which thoughts are necessarily indexed to certain kinds of behaviours. Roughly speaking, the behaviourist identifies thinking that the kitchen is on fire with a disposition to produce certain kinds of behaviours—such as uttering 'The kitchen is on fire'—in the appropriate circumstances. But although identifying thoughts with behavioural dispositions would solve the problem of other minds, the price that one pays for this solution is too steep, for it is highly implausible to suppose that all thoughts can be correlated with particular behavioural dispositions in the way that the behaviourists envisaged. In his book *Verbal Behavior*, the psychologist B.F. Skinner recalls a dinner party at which the philosopher Alfred North Whitehead challenged him to provide a behavioural analysis of the thought 'No black scorpion is falling upon this table'. Needless to say, the challenge went unmet.

Although behaviourism has few contemporary advocates, many theorists share the behaviourist's conviction that the identity of a creature's thoughts is essentially connected to its perceptual and behavioural environment. This proposal lies at the heart of functionalism. Functionalists conceive of thoughts as internal states that mediate between input states and output states of various kinds. A particular thought—say, the thought that the kitchen is on fire—is an internal state that is apt to have certain kinds of causes (e.g., seeing smoke emerge from the kitchen; feeling the heat given off by the flames) and is in turn apt to have certain kinds of effects (e.g., looking for the fire escape; calling the emergency services). The functionalist takes the identity of a thought to be fixed by the functional role that it plays within the cognitive economy of the subject in which it occurs.

The functionalist perspective on thought is an improvement on behaviourism in two ways. Firstly, it holds that the identity of a thought is fixed not only by its behavioural effects, but also by its perceptual causes. Secondly, the functionalist conception of thought is fundamentally holistic. Whereas the behaviourist takes thoughts to be *individually* characterizable in terms of particular behavioural dispositions, the functionalist holds that the identity of a thought is determined by the role that it plays within the overall psychological economy in which it occurs. Importantly, this economy will include other thoughts. This explains the fact that the same thought can have very different behavioural manifestations. For example, thinking that the kitchen is on fire will lead some people to attempt to flee the kitchen and others (e.g. firefighters) to attempt to enter it.

So, there is a clear contrast between the behaviourist account of thoughts and the functionalist account of thoughts. There is also a clear contrast between the functionalist account of thought and the Cartesian account. Whereas the Cartesian conceives of thoughts as purely private states—items whose identity is independent of any publicly accessible states of affairs—the functionalist holds that the identity of a thought depends on publicly accessible facts in the form of the subject's perceptual environment and behavioural responses. Because of this, functionalism is able to prevent the kind of scepticism about other minds that threatens the Cartesian view from taking hold.

Not only does functionalism provide us with a prophylactic against the problem of other minds, it also explains why our access to the thoughts of others is often provisional and uncertain. Even very extensive information about a creature's perceptual context and behavioural dispositions may fail to determine a unique assignment of thoughts to them. ('Did she say that because she was embarrassed, or because she intended to insult him?') We are pretty good at identifying the thoughts of individuals we know well, and—more generally—of those with whom we share a common language and culture, but identifying the thoughts of those who belong to cultures that are radically unlike our own is often challenging, as anthropologists know only too well. Our shared humanity grounds the reliability of a certain range of mental-state ascriptions, but the further we move away from those who are 'near and dear' to us, the more uncertain our access to the thoughts of others becomes. Even more daunting are the challenges posed by identifying the thoughts of those who lack speech. We will consider such challenges in the next chapter.

Brain writing and mind reading

Until recently, our only access to the minds of others was via the interrogation of their behaviour. In recent decades, however, a novel form of 'mind reading' has emerged. The method in question is known as 'brain reading' or 'brain decoding', and involves ascribing thoughts to a person on the basis of information about their patterns of brain activity. In one study, the neuroscientist John-Dylan Haynes and colleagues presented two numbers to the participants (say, 3 and 7), and instructed them to either covertly add the numbers together or subtract one number from the other. Using data derived from functional neuroimaging, Haynes and colleagues were able to determine with up to 70 per cent accuracy whether the subjects would add or subtract the presented numbers.

The reliability of the brain-decoding technique that was employed in the Haynes study could be assessed by asking subjects what their mental states were, but brain-decoding techniques have also been deployed in contexts in which behavioural verification of this kind is rather more problematic. The neuroscientist Adrian Owen and colleagues have used these techniques to investigate whether patients in the vegetative state might nonetheless possess some capacity for thought. In one study, a vegetative-state patient was instructed to imagine herself either playing tennis or visiting the rooms of her home. Surprisingly, the patient showed neural activity in response to these instructions that was similar to that produced by cognitively unimpaired individuals. Owen and his colleagues concluded that the patient had consciously followed the instructions given to her. Although this interpretation of the data is controversial—a number of critics have accepted that these results provide us with evidence that the patient was processing information of some kind but they deny that we have reason to think that that information processing was conscious—it certainly raises the possibility that brain decoding might be able to detect signs of conscious thought that remain inaccessible to traditional 'mind-reading' methods.

What is the potential scope of these techniques? Is there any reason to think that neuroscientists might acquire the kind of access to one's mind that could rival one's own? Could one use these techniques to take the luck out of the guess-a-number game?

Although it is unwise to predict what science might (or might not) deliver, it is worth emphasizing the limitations of current 'brain-decoding' methods. Firstly, these studies artificially constrain the range of thoughts that subjects can entertain. In the Haynes study, subjects were instructed to either add the presented numbers or to subtract them; in the Owen study, the subject was instructed to either imagine herself playing tennis or to imagine herself walking around her house. But the range of thoughts that subjects can entertain in real-world contexts is not constrained in these ways, and thus the task of identifying a subject's thoughts in everyday life will be vastly more difficult than it is in laboratory conditions. Secondly, these studies employ previously established correlations between thoughts and types of neural activity. Despite what is sometimes claimed, they do not involve decoding the language of thought (indeed, they do not even presume that there *is* a language of thought). As a result, these techniques do not enable neuroscientists to identify thoughts that are not already included in the neuroscientist's database of correlations. In this respect, 'brain-reading' techniques are less impressive than the traditional behaviourally based mind-reading techniques that we use on an everyday basis, for we routinely employ such techniques to ascribe thoughts that we have not previously entertained.

Might developments in brain-decoding methods find ways of overcoming these limitations? Only time will tell. What we can say for now is that there is little chance that neuroscientists will any time soon acquire the kind of access to your thoughts that you possess.

From the outer to the inner (and back again)

I have argued that there is some truth to the Cartesian conception of thought: the access that one has to one's own thoughts differs not just in degree but also in kind from the access that one has to the thoughts of others. But does this mean that the essence of thought involves some kind of inner event—a performance on the stage of an inner Cartesian theatre? Perhaps not. There are conceptions of thought that are anti-Cartesian in spirit, and yet allow us to do justice to what truth there seems to be in the Cartesian picture.

Suppose that (complex, distinctively human) thought begins with a public symbol system of some kind. Perhaps the first thinkers used (say) counters of some kind to represent objects. For example, one bean might represent one source of water, two beans might represent two sources of water, and so on. By manipulating beans, a community of early hominids might be more easily able to track the distribution of water sources. In time, the use of counters to represent objects is supplemented with, and eventually supplanted by, the use of words. And once creatures are able to speak to each other they are able to speak to themselves, and a creature that is able to speak to itself may, in time, acquire the capacity to keep its thoughts to itself. The Cartesian regards thought as first and foremost an inner process—something that occurs in the 'shuttered room' of one's own mind—and is only made publicly available by some further act of communication. The picture that I have sketched here stands that view on its head, and holds that thought—at least distinctively human thought—has its roots in the publicly accessible space of perception and action.

On this view, a creature's thoughts are naturally manifest in its behaviour. Some creatures may never acquire the capacity to hide their thoughts; others may acquire that capacity only gradually. Consider how children learn to count. Counting is not an ability that children acquire by first mastering an internal language of thought which they must then translate into a natural language. Instead, children first learn to count by saying number words aloud or by pointing to their fingers and toes. Once they have mastered the ability to count in this way, children can then acquire the capacity to count to themselves, in the privacy of their own minds. A process that begins 'in the open' becomes internalized, and thus hidden from the view of others. (Perhaps the evolutionary driver for this process was deception—the need to keep one's thoughts to oneself.) And once we have learnt to keep our thoughts to ourselves we can play the guess-a-number game, plan surprise birthday parties, and plot the downfall of our rivals.

Chapter 4
Brute thought

> A dog can believe his master is at the door. But can he also
> believe that his master will come the day after tomorrow?
>
> Ludwig Wittgenstein, *Philosophical Investigations*

Can non-human animals think? If so, what kinds of thoughts can
they enjoy? Dogs might have beliefs and desires of certain kinds,
but can they entertain the possibility that something could be the
case or hope that it is the case? Whether or not non-human
animals are capable of thoughts of any kind, it is clear that there
are profound differences between the cognitive capacities of
humans and those of other species. What explains these
differences? Can they be fully explained by the most obvious
contrast between animals and ourselves—namely, the possession
of a natural language—or do non-linguistic factors play a role in
accounting for the gulf between our cognitive capacities and those
of other species? These questions animated discussion in
Aristotle's time, and they continue to generate debate today.

Preliminary challenges

A number of preliminary challenges confront the study of animal
thought. The first of these challenges concerns the very *possibility*
of animal thought. Is animal thought an open issue that is to be
settled by the normal methods of science, or are there principled

reasons for denying that non-linguistic creatures could ever think (as many theorists have argued)?

The most obvious strategy for arguing that language is required for thought would be to argue that language is required for one of the cognitive capacities associated with thought, such as the capacity to represent objects in their absence; the capacity to represent a wide range of objects and properties; or the capacity to represent one's environment in a systematic and open-ended manner. Is natural language required for any of these capacities? It is certainly plausible to suspect that natural language might *facilitate* the acquisition of these capacities. Indeed, there may even be biological constraints on cognitive architecture which prevent a creature from acquiring these capacities without first (or simultaneously) acquiring the capacity to understand language. But—the claims of many influential figures notwithstanding—there is no good a priori reason for assuming that these capacities demand the mastery of a public language. Thought does require a representational system of some sort, but it is an open question whether that system must take the form of a natural language or whether it could not instead be something akin to a 'language of thought'.

A second challenge is methodological: even if those who cannot speak can nonetheless think, how could we ever discover evidence of thought in such creatures? How can we determine what a creature is thinking—indeed, how can we even determine *that* a creature is thinking—if it cannot answer the questions that we put to it?

The first thing to note is that epistemic problems of this kind also confront the ascription of thoughts to creatures that *can* answer our questions. As the Mad Hatter pointed out to Alice, we do not always mean what we say, nor do we always say what we mean. The interpretation of speech is often tentative and provisional, and we rely on a host of background assumptions about a person's sincerity, their knowledge of the audience, and their grasp of the meaning of the words that they use in order to infer what they think from what they say. Furthermore, although non-verbal creatures cannot *tell* us what they are thinking, there are various ways in which we can get a fix on the contents of their thoughts. For example, we can look at the kinds of properties that they are differentially sensitive to. Suppose that we are wondering whether Fido can think about squirrels. If Fido distinguishes squirrels from other objects in his environment, then we may have grounds for ascribing thoughts about squirrels to Fido. We might, for example, be justified in thinking that Fido believes that there is a squirrel up a tree. (Of course, we should not require that Fido is able to distinguish squirrels from everything else before being ready to ascribe squirrel-related thoughts to him. After all, *we* cannot distinguish squirrels from certain kinds of squirrel-impersonating robots, yet there is no doubt that we can think about squirrels.) Arguably, the difference between verbal behaviour and non-verbal behaviour is one of degree and not one of kind.

So, there seems to be no reason to dismiss out of hand the possibility that non-linguistic creatures might possess the capacity for thought, nor is there good reason to assume that such thoughts as they might have would be beyond our powers to detect. Language may enable us to ascribe thoughts to a creature with a precision that cannot be obtained in its absence, but it would be a mistake to conclude that we can never know the thoughts of a non-linguistic creature.

Mathematics, sociology, and psychology

Where might we look to find evidence of thought in a species? We could consider its navigational capacities, for navigational prowess often involves representing the temporal and spatial features of one's environment in complex and systematic ways. Alternatively, we could look at its tool-making capacities, for turning an object into a tool requires a grasp of its causal properties. There are rich literatures on these topics, but we will focus here on three other domains in which evidence of animal thought can be found: the domain of numbers, the domain of social relations, and the domain of mentality.

Studies have indicated that a great many species have some capacity to track the mathematical properties of objects in their environment. In one experiment, the psychologists Russell Church and Warren Meck exposed rats to both tones and flashes of light. The rats were initially trained to press the left lever when they heard two tones and the right lever when they heard four tones. The rats were also taught to press the left lever in response to two flashes of light and the right lever in response to four flashes of light. What would the rats do when presented with one tone and one flash of light? They immediately pressed the left lever, indicating that they had coded the stimulus as 'two events', and they immediately pressed the right lever in response to two tones and two flashes of light, indicating that they had coded that stimulus as 'four events'.

A number of species can also compare numerical quantities with some degree of accuracy. The primatologist Duane Rumbaugh and his colleagues showed chimpanzees two trays of chocolate chips, of which they could choose only one. Each tray contained two piles of chocolate chips. For example, one tray might contain a three-chip pile and a four-chip pile, while the other tray might contain a seven-chip pile and a two-chip pile. Chimpanzees like chocolate chips, and thus they were faced with the problem of determining which tray had more chips on it. In order to solve this problem, the chimpanzees needed to first sum the two piles that appeared on each tray, and then work out which of the two trays had the larger number of chips. Although chimpanzees faltered when the overall number of chips on each tray were very similar, they were generally highly accurate at choosing the tray which had the larger number of chips.

In fact, there is evidence that chimpanzees can even grasp simple fractions. In one experiment, the primatologists David Premack and Guy Woodruff trained chimpanzees to identify halves of objects. For example, when shown half a glass of milk as a target object, the chimpanzees choose half an apple and would ignore three-quarters of an apple. Premack and Woodruff then presented the chimpanzees with an image of a quarter of an apple and an image of half a glass of milk. The animals were able to combine these two images and match them to an image that represented three-quarters, indicating that they possessed an intuitive grasp of fractions.

Taken as a whole, the evidence suggests that a number of species—and indeed human infants from about six months of age—have the capacity both to represent small quantities (one-ness, two-ness, three-ness, and greater-than-three-ness) in exact ways and to represent larger quantities (that is, quantities above three) in approximate terms. These representations are thought-like insofar as they are, to varying degrees, stimulus-independent. However, neither non-human animals nor human infants appear to be capable of representing larger numbers in exact terms. As we shall see in the next chapter, that capacity may require the grasp of number terms.

Let us turn now to a second domain in which evidence of animal thought has been obtained—that of social relations. Social rank plays an important role in many species, and it is vital that an individual knows not only its own place in the social universe but is also able to track the social status of the other members of its group. Some of the most intensive research on social cognition in non-human primates has been conducted by the primatologists Dorothy Cheney and Robert Seyfarth on baboons. The social world of a female baboon involves a two-tiered hierarchy in which whole families are ranked relative to each other and the females within each family are ranked relative to each other. This ranking—which is fluid—plays a pivotal role in structuring the interactions that a baboon will have with the other members of its troop, and thus it is no surprise to discover that baboons have complex representations of their social world. For example, a baboon may be more surprised by a sequence of calls that represents a subordinate threatening a dominant from a different family than it is by a sequence of calls that represents an analogous intra-familial conflict, even when the difference in overall rank order is identical.

There are a number of respects in which a baboon's understanding of its social world manifests the features of thought. Firstly, a baboon's grasp of its social universe is not coupled to any particular perceptual modality but is independent of its immediate perceptual environment. For example, a baboon's interpretation of a series of vocalizations made by another baboon may depend both on what it hears and on what it sees. Secondly, the properties that are being tracked (such as being of subordinate status) are not directly manifest in the creature's environment, but require the deployment of a theory that determines the kinds of physical and behavioural properties that affect a baboon's social status. A human being who did not have such an understanding would not be able to track the social relations between the members of the baboon troop in the way that a baboon can. Thirdly, a baboon's understanding of its social environment appears to be reasonably systematic and open-ended. A baboon can represent a great number of possible relations between the members of its troop. It can represent not just those relations that it expects, but also those relations that are unexpected and incongruous. Taken together, these features provide good justification for describing the baboon's representation of its social world as a form of thought.

The members of certain non-human species might qualify as amateur sociologists, but do they also qualify as amateur psychologists? We have sophisticated capacities for tracking mental states—both our own and those of others—but do the members of other species share these capacities?

Let us begin with what would seem to be a fairly primitive aspect of mentality: the notion of a visual perspective. Are animals able to determine what another creature can see—and thus, perhaps, what they know—on the basis of information about its direction of gaze? Primates, at least, appear to have *some* grip on the connection between seeing and knowing. For example, primates will follow the gaze of another creature in order to locate the object of its attention; they will also remove prized food items from the line of sight of other animals. But do primates really understand the notion of a visual perspective, or have they just learnt the behavioural correlations that are associated with an animal's visual perspective, such as the fact that animals who look at a desirable food item tend to eat it?

A series of experiments conducted by the primatologists Daniel Povinelli and Timothy Eddy seemed to suggest that chimpanzees have only a behavioural grasp of visual perspective. In these experiments, chimpanzees could choose to beg for food from one or other of two people. One of the persons could see the chimpanzee, but although the other person was facing the chimpanzee she could not see it, either because she had a bucket on her head or because she was wearing a blindfold (Figure 2). Povinelli and Eddy found that chimpanzees were no more likely to beg from the experimenter who could see them than they were to beg from the experimenter who could not see them, which suggests that the chimpanzees had failed to grasp the connection between seeing and knowing.

This result is remarkable, but it should be noted that it tests chimpanzees on a task that may fail to play to their strengths. Wild chimpanzees usually compete for access to food, and it is not common for them to acquire food by begging. With this in mind, the evolutionary anthropologist Brian Hare and his colleagues wondered whether chimpanzees might demonstrate that they understand the relationship between seeing and knowing if they were tested in a paradigm that involved competition for food.

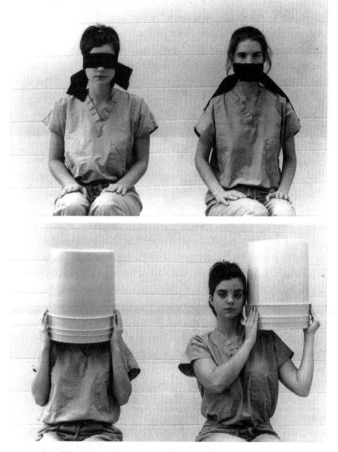

2. **Testing chimpanzees' understanding of seeing**

Hare and his colleagues explored this possibility by placing a
dominant chimpanzee and a subordinate chimpanzee in a room
containing two pieces of food. One food item could be seen by
both chimpanzees, but the other was visible only to the
subordinate chimpanzee. Dominant chimpanzees typically take all

the food that is available to them and punish subordinates who challenge them. Thus, if the subordinate chimpanzee understood the connection between seeing and knowing—and, in particular, the connection between *not* seeing and *not* knowing—then it should preferentially target the food item that was placed behind the barrier. That is precisely what happened.

How far might the 'mind-reading' abilities of other primates extend? Might primates have the capacity to monitor their own states of mind? There is some suggestive evidence in this regard. Work by David Smith and his colleagues has indicated that monkeys may have the capacity to monitor their own states of certainty and uncertainty. In these studies, monkeys learned to control a joystick which enabled them to respond to questions on a test of visual discrimination. When the monkeys answered correctly they received food, but when their answers were incorrect they had to wait for the next trial—which they did not like doing. The monkeys then learned that by pressing a special icon they could 'opt out' of a trial. Opting out of a trial meant that the monkey did not receive any food, but it also meant that the next trial was not delayed. The monkeys' use of the 'opt out' icon suggested that they were tracking how difficult they thought each particular trial was, for they opted out only on difficult trials (that is, on trials in which they were more likely to get the wrong answer and thus suffer a delay). Interestingly, dolphins also appear to have the capacity to monitor their own degrees of certainty in this way.

So, there is evidence that a number of non-human species are able to represent a variety of domains in thought-like ways. However, what we know about animal thought pales into insignificance when compared with what we do not know. What kinds of propositional attitudes might non-human animals be capable of enjoying? Animals can have beliefs, desires, and intentions, but do they also possess the ability to merely *entertain* a thought? And what about episodes of conscious thinking? Do animals enjoy trains of conscious thought the direction of which they actively guide, or is their conscious thought life—such as it is—purely passive? And what is the range of non-human thought? Are the members of any other species capable of self-conscious thought—are they able to think of themselves *as* themselves—or is the capacity for self-consciousness uniquely human? These and many other questions concerning animal thought remain unanswered at present.

Distinctively human thought

We may not be the only species to qualify as thinkers, but no species comes even close to matching the range and sophistication of human thought. The fact that we have given ourselves the title of *homo sapiens* is not an act of hubris, but due recognition of the fact that we are the only species to have created the social institutions necessary for government and religion, the only species to have developed complex tools and technologies, and the only species to have produced a sophisticated material culture. The members of other species—not to mention the immature members of our own species—may have some capacity for thought, but that capacity is profoundly impoverished relative to that enjoyed by mature human beings. What accounts for the uniqueness of human thought?

One striking feature of human thought involves our ability to disengage the focus of thought from that of our perceptual attention. We are able to look at one thing whilst thinking about something else entirely. By contrast, if one wants to get a fix on what an animal (or prelinguistic child) is thinking about, one need only determine the object of its perceptual attention.

The ability to decouple one's thoughts from one's immediate environment may be facilitated by (and perhaps even require) the use of symbols. Consider the following anecdote regarding Sheba, an adult chimpanzee who had been trained to use symbols (numerals) to represent items, and Sarah, another chimpanzee.

Sheba and Sarah were sitting in front of two plates of treats. The experiment was structured such that Sheba got the larger plate of treats only when she pointed to the smaller plate. (When Sheba pointed to the larger plate of treats it was given instead to Sarah.) Although Sheba clearly understood what she needed to do in order to get the larger plate of treats (which she clearly wanted!) she was not able to overcome her instinctive tendency to point towards the larger (and thus more desirable) plate of treats until the plates were covered over and numerals representing the number of treats that each plate contained were placed on top of them. The presence of the symbols allowed Sheba to use her knowledge of the rule ('If I want the larger plate I have to point to the smaller one') to point to the smaller plate and thus acquire her goal.

Another example of the transformative power of symbols is provided by a study of chimpanzees who were trained to use symbols (plastic tags) to represent the relations of sameness and difference. For example, a pair of cups might be associated with a red triangle to indicate that they are objects of the same kind, whereas a cup and a shoe might be associated with a blue circle to indicate the difference between them. After training, the chimpanzees who had been trained in the use of these symbols—and only those chimpanzees—were able to use the tags to appreciate relations of higher-order sameness and difference. In other words, they were able to appreciate that two pairs (such as cup–cup and cup–shoe) instantiate the relation of difference, since the first pair exhibits the sameness relations and the latter pair exhibits the difference relation. The authors of the study suggested that the symbols enabled the chimpanzees to perform this task because by visualizing the tags they could transform the higher-order task (of determining the relations between objects) into a first-order task of determining whether the symbols associated with each pair were the same.

As the philosopher Andy Clark has remarked, 'experience with external tags and labels thus enables the brain itself...to solve problems whose level of complexity and abstraction would otherwise leave us baffled'. Perhaps, as Wittgenstein thought, a dog might need to master the use of symbols in order to believe that his master or mistress will come the day after tomorrow. And perhaps the same point applies to the question of whether animals can enjoy propositional attitudes such as hope. A dog may have the capacity to hope for something that is immediately suggested by its perceptual environment—such as the possibility that it might receive food scraps from the table—but the hope for things unseen (or unsmelt) might require a symbol to act as a proxy for the object of thought.

A second respect in which human thought may be distinctive concerns the ability to engage in what the psychologist Endel Tulving has dubbed 'mental time travel'—the capacity to remember the past and anticipate the future in a distinctively 'first-personal' manner. The capacity for mental time travel extends into the past ('I can recall visiting Darjeeling as a child') and into the future ('I can anticipate what it might be like to return to Darjeeling now'). The projective component of mental time travel—being able to imagine oneself in a certain type of situation—is central to planning. It is the capacity for projective imagination that enables one to recognize that the mild discomfort of a dental check-up is outweighed by the fact that it enables one to avoid the more serious pain of future dental problems. Projective imagination also plays an important role in tool construction by enabling one to anticipate the consequences of an action.

Is mental time travel uniquely human? The question is currently unresolved. Other species certainly produce some of the behavioural manifestations of mental time travel. Consider the caching behaviour of scrub jays. In a series of experiments, the psychologists Nicola Clayton and Anthony Dickinson gave worms and peanuts to scrub jays to cache in different locations. Scrub jays prefer fresh worms to peanuts, but they prefer peanuts to worms that have been cached for some time (and may have become inedible). The experiments demonstrated that scrub jays remember not just *where* they cached the food that they had been given but also *when* they had cached it, for they retrieved freshly cached worms before retrieving peanuts and they retrieved peanuts before retrieving worms that had been cached for some time.

Does this mean that scrub jays have the capacity for 'mental time travel'? Perhaps not. Rather than 'consciously reliving' their acts of caching the worms and peanuts, it is possible that the scrub jays are acting on the basis of a kind of propositional memory: they might know when an act of caching occurred without being able to remember the act itself 'from the inside', so to speak. This might be thought, but it would be a very different kind of thought from that which we enjoy in virtue of our capacity for mental time travel.

A third respect in which human thought is unique concerns its relationship to the environment. The environment in which human thought takes place radically enhances its reach and its robustness. We augment the fragile forms of 'direct' control that we possess over the direction of our thoughts with tools of various kinds, the most powerful of which is natural language. By putting our thoughts into words we are able to take a step back from them and subject them to critical evaluation. Plato's characterization of thought as 'the soul talking to itself' might not have been quite right, but there is good reason to suppose that much distinctively human thought involves—or is at least facilitated by—inner speech and other linguistic tricks. Many of us do our best thinking with a pen (or iPad) in hand.

Human thought does not merely occur in a linguistic environment, it also occurs in a social environment. We are born into a community of thinkers, and we learn to think by being guided by those who are experts in this craft. Indeed, it is no exaggeration to regard childhood as an extended apprenticeship in the business of thinking. We learn both *what* to think and—perhaps more importantly—*how* to think. As with all true apprenticeships, the majority of this instruction is implicit rather than explicit. Rather than being taught a set of formal rules for the 'direction of the mind', we learn how to think by being provided with examples of good thinking. The German philosopher Immanuel Kant described such examples as the *gängelwagen* of thought, where a *gängelwagen* is a walking frame or go-kart that is harnessed to an infant in order to help it learn to walk (Figure 3). Just as the *gängelwagen* enables a child to master the art of walking, so too examples enable it to master the art of thinking.

Central to this developmental trajectory is the practice of social referencing. From the age of one, human infants are acutely sensitive to the attentional focus of adults. Not only do infants 'tune in' to the attentional focus of adults, they also attempt to get adults to 'tune in' to their attentional focus. The social scaffolding of thought is not restricted to infancy and childhood but is present throughout our lives. We criticize a person's thoughts by describing them as 'irrational' or 'reckless'; we praise them as 'creative' or 'insightful'. The social evaluation of our thinking acts as a corrective to idiosyncratic thought, allowing us to consider aspects of an issue that we may have missed. In conversation with others we find ourselves with thoughts we did not know we were capable of, relying on the stimulation provided by the other person's prodding and probing to keep our thoughts on track. Indeed, there is evidence that groups generate better-quality thoughts when they foster a spirit of healthy debate and dissent among their members. The social dimension of human thought appears to be completely absent from the cognitive lives of other species. Even chimpanzees—our closest relatives—do not point or produce any other kind of communicative signal that might encourage their fellow chimpanzees to enter into their states of mind.

But perhaps most importantly of all, the mechanisms of cultural transmission allow the best thoughts of one generation to be passed on to the generations that follow. Unlike other species, whose cognitive breakthroughs have to be rediscovered anew by every successive generation, we are able build on the cognitive

3. A child's *gängelwagen*

foundations laid down by our ancestors. We inherit not just the contents of their thoughts, but—even more importantly—we also inherit methods for generating, evaluating, and communicating thoughts. Of course, as with any inheritance there is no guarantee that the cognitive tools that we acquire will always be in good working order, but there is little doubt that we gain more from this arrangement than we lose by it.

Chapter 5
'They don't think like we do'

Once there was a man of Chu'u selling shields and halberds. In praising his shields he said, 'My shields are so solid that nothing can penetrate them.' Again, in praising his halberds, he said, 'My halberds are so sharp that they can penetrate anything.' In response to his words somebody asked, 'How about using your halberds to pierce through your shields?' To this the man could not give any reply.

Han Fei Tzu, 3rd century BCE

The ancient Greek philosopher Aristotle took the capacity for rational thought to be a defining feature of human nature, a feature that distinguishes human beings from other animals. However, Aristotle also held that this capacity is not everywhere the same, and that Greek modes of thought were superior to those of other cultures. According to Aristotle, although non-Greeks could understand the reasoning of others, they lacked the capacity to generate rational thoughts of their own. Aristotle's views concerning the superiority of Greek modes of thought would have few contemporary advocates, but the question he raised remains a live one: are the structures of thought fundamentally invariant across changes of cultural context, or is there some truth in the oft-heard remark that 'they'—that is, those on the 'other' side of the world—do not think like 'we' do?

For the most part psychologists tend to adopt a universalist conception of human thought, according to which the modes of thought are fundamentally the same in all societies. Anthropologists, on the other hand, tend to be sympathetic to particularist conceptions of human thought, according to which the modes of thought differ in important ways from one society to another. Rather than emphasizing the commonalities in thought between the members of different societies (as psychologists typically do), anthropologists tend to emphasize the contrasts between them.

As we will see, adjudicating the debate between universalists and particularists is far from straightforward. Part of the problem is that the very terms in which the debate is posed are somewhat murky. What exactly does it mean for two societies to differ in the modes of thought that they employ? Would particularism be vindicated by the discovery that there is variation in the modes of thought that different societies *tend* to exhibit, or would it be vindicated only by showing that there is variation in the modes of thought that different societies *can* exhibit? A further source of uncertainty surrounding this debate is empirical: we know surprisingly little about how human beings in general think. The vast majority of psychological research into reasoning involves only American undergraduates, and American undergraduates constitute a very small—and quite possibly unrepresentative—sample of the human family. We would be justified in applying the results of these studies to human beings in general only if we already knew that the modes of human thought were everywhere the same. For their part, anthropologists provide detailed case studies of the modes of thought employed in a particular culture, but it is often unclear how the studies that are conducted in one culture should be compared with those conducted in another culture. In short, significant challenges face anyone looking to take the measure of this debate.

We will attempt to navigate these murky waters by focusing on three questions. Firstly, to what extent might there be socially based variation in the contents of thought? Secondly, do the members of some societies have a tendency to employ patterns of inference that the members of other societies do not—and perhaps cannot—employ? Thirdly, how might the relationship between thought and language bear on the debate between universalist and particularist conceptions of human thought?

The contents of thought

It is apparent to any casual observer of human nature that societies have different conceptions of reality. Societies differ in their religious beliefs, their philosophical views, and their moral and political outlooks. To take just one example of such differences, consider the question of whether non-human animals might be legally responsible for their actions: although 'we' might think it obvious that an animal cannot be held legally responsible for its actions, the legal code of ancient Athens contained statues for the regulation of animal trials, and such trials were not unknown in medieval Europe.

So, it is clear that human beings can have different—sometimes very different—conceptions of the world. What is less clear is whether these differences in thought are limited to what—with apologies to non-human animals—we might describe as 'marginal' aspects of reality, or whether they also characterize 'core' features of thought—that is, features of thought that govern our everyday lives. Let us consider this question in light of what we know about two such domains: thinking about space and thinking about minds.

It is possible to think about spatial relations in two ways: egocentrically and geocentrically. Egocentric conceptions of space employ a frame of reference that is focused on oneself. For example, an egocentric conception of a tree's location might represent the tree as lying *to the left of* the house. (From another perspective that same tree might be represented as lying *to the right of* the house.) Geocentric conceptions of space, by contrast, employ a frame of reference that is centred on the earth. For example, a geocentric conception of a tree's location might represent the tree as lying *to the north of* the house. Might societies differ in the degree to which they privilege one or other of these two ways of thinking about space?

The psycholinguist Stephen Levinson has argued that they do. Levinson and his collaborators have approached this question by comparing the ways in which the speakers of different languages think about space. Some languages privilege egocentric descriptions of space. For example, although both English and Dutch support the capacity for geocentric descriptions—indeed, I used such a description in the previous paragraph!—the speakers of these languages strongly favour egocentric terms when describing the spatial relations between objects in their immediate environment. Other languages, by contrast, strongly favour a geocentric frame of reference. For example, speakers of Tzeltal, a Mayan language spoken in Mexico, rarely (if ever) use terms corresponding to 'left' and 'right'. Instead of asking someone to pass the cup on their left, Tzeltal speakers will ask for the cup 'to the north' of the person facing them.

Might this linguistic contrast be accompanied by a corresponding contrast in how the speakers of these languages think about space? Levinson and his colleagues explored this question by comparing the spatial reasoning of Dutch speakers with that of Tzeltal speakers. Participants were shown a card on a table with a red dot to the left/north of a blue dot. The participants were then rotated 180 degrees to face a second table, where they were instructed to choose from among a set of cards the one that was 'the same' as the card that they had just seen. One of the cards from which they could choose featured an array with the same egocentric (that is, left–right) orientation as the target card but a different geocentric (that is, north–south) orientation, whereas another card had the same geocentric orientation but a different egocentric orientation. Tzeltal speakers overwhelmingly chose the card with the same *geocentric* orientation as the target, whereas Dutch speakers overwhelmingly chose the card with the same *egocentric* orientation as the target. On the basis of these and other findings, Levinson suggests that speakers of geocentric languages think about space in ways that are fundamentally different from those employed by the speakers of egocentric languages.

This claim, however, is not unproblematic. For one thing, it is possible that the contrasting performance of Tzeltal speakers and Dutch speakers can be explained by supposing that they made different assumptions about what counts as 'the same' in this context. Perhaps the Tzeltal speakers assumed that they had been instructed to match the target to a card that had the same geocentric structure, whereas the Dutch speakers assumed that they had been instructed to match the target to a card with the same egocentric structure. More importantly, there is evidence that Tzeltal speakers *can* think about spatial relations egocentrically. The psychologists Peggy Li and Anna Papafragou tested this possibility by presenting Tzeltal speakers with problems that could be solved only by egocentric reasoning. They found that participants were as adept at solving these problems as they were at solving problems that required geocentric reasoning. Tzeltal speakers may not *talk* in egocentric terms, but they seem to be perfectly capable of *thinking* egocentrically.

Let us turn now to another core aspect of human thought: thought about the mind. Arguably there is more cultural variation in how we think about the mind than there is in how we think about space. For example, in some cultures, the dead are taken to be able to influence the thoughts and behaviour of the living, whereas such an assumption is not typically made in contemporary Western societies. There is also cultural variation in how one person's mind is thought to be able to influence another person's mind. In contemporary Western society it is generally assumed that one can influence someone else's thoughts only via a perceptual channel of some kind (for example, by means of speaking to them), whereas other cultures regard some people as having the power to influence the minds of other agents without any kind of perceptual contact. Again, some cultures assume that human perception is limited to the five commonly acknowledged sensory channels, whereas other cultures allow that certain individuals have powers of extrasensory perception, and are able to 'see' and 'hear' things that are beyond the reach of normal perception. Indeed, there are cultures in which a person's emotional responses are thought to be capable of causing illness in other people. For example, the Micronesian Ifaluk believe that missing one's relatives can cause those relatives to become ill.

There is also evidence that the members of different cultures tend to think about the relationship between agents and their environments in subtly different ways. In the 1970s social psychologists noticed that most people overemphasize the degree to which the behaviours of people are manifestations of their character traits—underlying features of their personality—as opposed to being caused by contingent features of their environment. For example, people tend to assume that someone's nervous behaviour in the context of a job interview is evidence that they have a nervous disposition, overlooking the fact that job interviews are unusually stressful environments that agitate even the most unflappable of individuals. The tendency of people to emphasize trait-based explanations of behaviour at the expense of environmental factors appeared to be so robust that it was dubbed the 'fundamental attribution error'. However, recent research has suggested that the so-called 'fundamental attribution error' may be far from fundamental. Rather than characterizing human beings in general, the attribution error appears to be most pronounced in societies that place an emphasis on individual autonomy, and it is much less robust—and perhaps even altogether absent—in cultures that emphasize collective action and conformity to social norms.

So, there are some differences in the ways in which the members of different cultures think about minds. Nonetheless, these differences are likely to be exceptions that stand out against a background of cross-cultural uniformity. As far as we know, humans everywhere explain both their own behaviour and that of their fellow creatures by appeal to belief, desire, intention, perception, emotion, memory, and imagination. Although there is some variation in the age at which the children in different cultures acquire these concepts, no one has yet uncovered a society in which a robust understanding of mentalistic categories is not firmly in place by the end of childhood. At least as far as space and mentality are concerned, cross-cultural differences in thought—such as they are—seem to be exceptions to a more general framework of cross-cultural uniformity.

Modes of inference

Let us turn from thoughts to thinking. Might the members of one society reason in a fundamentally different way from the members of another society? Indeed, might the members of some societies simply fail to grasp the force of certain modes of inference?

Influential figures in the history of anthropology have answered these questions in the affirmative. In his book *How Natives Think*, published in 1910, the French anthropologist Lucien Lévy-Brühl suggested that pre-literate peoples have little aptitude for logical thought, and that the members of such societies were 'uncultivated in following a chain of reasoning which is in the slightest degree abstract'. In the 1930s the Russian psychologist Alexander Luria put these claims to the test by examining whether a group of illiterate peasants in Uzbekistan were able to grasp the logical relations between propositions. In one set of studies, he told the peasants that in the far north all the bears are white, and that Novaya Zemlya is in the far north. He then asked the peasants what colour the bears are in Novaya Zemlya. Fewer than 30 per cent of the peasants drew the appropriate inference. Some of them responded that they did not know what colour the bears were. One peasant was reported to have said, 'You've seen them, you know. I haven't seen them, so how could I say?' By contrast, members of the same society who had received formal schooling had no difficulty solving the reasoning problems that Luria put to them.

Luria concluded that the peasants had impoverished reasoning skills, and drew the more general conclusion that formal schooling is required for the mastery of abstract reasoning. Now, although it is certainly very plausible to think that formal tuition fosters an individual's capacity for abstract reasoning, it is far from clear that Luria's studies show that those who have not been formally schooled are *incapable* of abstract reasoning.

Two points need to be kept in mind in considering Luria's results. Firstly, conscious thought is tiring and effortful, especially when one is considering unfamiliar topics. The fact that the peasants that Luria interviewed performed so poorly may have had more to do with their levels of motivation—the degree to which they could see the point of expending effort on questions that had no obvious impact on their lives—than their capacity to grasp the arguments presented to them. Secondly, as Geoffrey Lloyd has pointed out, in most cultures the only questions that people pose are those to which they do not know the answer. In light of this, one might wonder whether the peasants might not have taken Luria's question ('What colour are the bears in Novaya Zemlya?') to reveal his ignorance about the colour of bears in the far north, and thus to cast doubt on his previous assertion—an assertion which is universal in form and thus difficult to conclusively verify—that all the bears in the far north are white. Indeed, the peasants may have worried that they would be seen as gullible if they simply accepted Luria's claims. After all, they themselves had not been to the far north, and Luria had not provided any evidence in support of his claims: why should they take them at face value? More recent studies of reasoning in non-literate societies have attempted to address these concerns by asking participants to reason about states of affairs that occur on an imaginary planet. Posing the questions in this manner leads to improved performance, suggesting that their poor performance on 'non-hypothetical' problems can be accounted for by the kinds of pragmatic factors mentioned above, and may not reflect an absolute inability to engage in 'abstract' or 'decontextualized' thought.

In recent years the debate between universalist and particularist accounts of human inference has focused not on the contrast between literate and non-literate societies, but on the contrast between East and West. For a number of years the psychologist Richard Nisbett and his collaborators have argued that there are robust differences between the ways that East Asians (that is, Japanese, Chinese, and Koreans) think and the ways that Westerners think. Nisbett and colleagues characterize these differences by saying that East Asians tend to think 'holistically' whereas Westerners tend to think 'analytically'. What does it mean to say that East Asians think holistically and Westerners think analytically? According to Nisbett and colleagues, East Asians tend to place more weight on the contextual aspects of a situation whereas Westerners tend to focus on its focal elements; East Asians tend to group objects on the basis of their relations whereas Westerners tend to group objects in terms of their membership of a common category; and East Asians tend to reason on the basis of similarity whereas Westerners tend to reason on the basis of rules.

Nisbett and his collaborators provide a range of evidence in favour of these claims. In one study, American and Japanese students were shown eight animated colour vignettes (see Figure 4 for a black-and-white illustration). Each scene contained a number of focal objects in the form of large, bright, and quickly moving fish, and a number of non-focal objects, such as rocks, bubbles, and slowly moving animals. After being presented with the scenes for brief periods, subjects were asked to report what they had seen.

Although the American and Japanese students made about an equal number of references to the fish, the Japanese students made about twice as many references to the background objects. In addition, whereas Japanese students generally began by describing the scene as a whole ('It looks like a pond'), the American students generally began by describing the focal objects ('There was a big fish, maybe a trout, moving to the left').

In another study, college students were presented with sets of three words—such as 'panda', 'monkey', and 'banana'—and asked which two of the three words were most closely related. In general, the American students grouped 'panda' and 'monkey' together, indicating that they preferred to categorize objects on the basis of their shared membership in a common category, whereas the East Asian students tended to group 'monkey' and 'banana' together, indicating that they preferred to categorize objects on the basis of their relations.

4. An example of an animated vignette

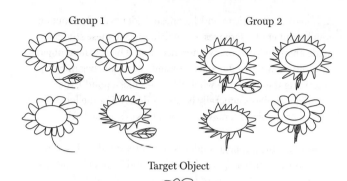

Group 1   Group 2

Target Object

5. Family resemblance versus rule-based categorization

A third study examined the inductive practices of East Asian and American students. The students were presented with a display that contained a target object at the bottom and two groups of objects at the top. The students were then asked to say which of the two groups of objects the target object was 'most similar to' or 'belonged with'.

There are two ways in which one might answer this question. Adopting a 'family resemblance' approach, one might match the target to the flowers on the left, for on the whole the target has most in common with these objects. Adopting a rule-based approach would lead one to match the target with the objects on the right, for there is a simple feature that the target shares with all of these objects: it has a straight stem. The majority of East Asian students categorized the target object on the basis of family resemblance, whereas the majority of European Americans categorized the target on the basis of the rule. (Interestingly, the performance of Asian Americans was intermediate between that of the East Asian students and the European American students.)

These studies are certainly thought provoking, but do they show that Easterners and Westerners 'reason in qualitatively different ways', as Nisbett claims? There are grounds for caution.

Firstly, the contrast between 'Eastern' and 'Western' modes of thought emerges only when one looks at the performance of groups. Many East Asian students produce responses that are typical of American students and vice versa. Secondly, there is little correlation between the degree to which an individual's performance on various tasks is holistic; in other words, many individuals reason 'holistically' in some contexts but not others. This suggests that the very distinction between these two modes of thought is rather problematic. Thirdly, these studies focus on undergraduates, and the ways in which the undergraduates within a society think may not be representative of the ways in which the members of that society in general think. Finally, to the extent that the reasoning practices of East Asian students differ from those of American students, these differences appear not to be fixed but are easily reversed. Just as American students can be readily primed to pair 'monkey' with 'banana', so too East Asian students can be readily primed to pair 'monkey' with 'panda'; and just as East Asian students can be led to categorize on the basis of rules, so too American students can be led to categorize on the basis of family resemblance. In other words, even if East Asians and Westerners tend to *prioritise* different cognitive strategies, they appear to have the same set of inferential strategies at their disposal. Certainly analytical arguments are not unknown in the history of Chinese thought, as the vignette that functions as the epigraph for this chapter illustrates.

Language and thought

Another aspect of the debate between particularists and universalists concerns the relationship between thought and language. There is good reason to expect cross-cultural differences in thought if—as many theorists have argued—the structure of thought is modulated by that of language, for societies obviously differ in the languages that they speak. But *is* the structure of thought modulated by the structure of language?

Of the many disputed questions concerning the nature of thought this is perhaps the most disputed of all. Although it is generally agreed that the mastery of *a* natural language has a transformative effect on thought (as we noted in the previous chapter), there is anything but general agreement about whether, how, and to what degree the differences between languages bear on the structure of thought. Some theorists regard the effects of language on thought as deep and profound, while others hold that the differences between languages are negligible as far as thought is concerned. As with many debates, the truth is likely to lie somewhere in the middle.

The claim that the structural features of a language play an important role in shaping thought is known as Whorfianism, in honour of the anthropological linguist Benjamin Whorf, who brought the view to prominence in the middle of the last century. Until recently, Whorfianism was not looked upon with a great deal of favour within cognitive science. One reason for this derives from the research conducted by Brent Berlin and Paul Kay in the 1960s on cross-cultural differences in colour perception. Berlin and Kay found that although languages differ in the number of colour terms they employ, there appear to be cross-cultural universals in the structure of colour terminology. If a language has just two colour terms then those terms will refer to black and white; if a language has just three colour terms then the third term will invariably refer to red; and if a language has more than three colour terms then the additional terms will refer to either green, blue, or yellow. This suggests that if there is any influence between the structure of language and that of the mind then it is the latter which influences the former rather than vice versa.

Although this finding was widely taken to show that thought is independent of language, that response now seems to have been somewhat premature. For one thing, recent evidence has suggested that colour perception might not be completely free of linguistic influence. For example, studies have found that the contrast between the perception of light blue and dark blue is more marked in speakers of Russian, a language in which the contrast between light blue and dark blue is marked by distinct terms, than it is for speakers of English, in which both colours are described as shades of blue. But perhaps more importantly, it is obviously a mistake to conclude that language has no effect on thought just because it has no effect on colour perception. After all, if language has any effects on mental structure, it is a priori more likely that these effects will be found in those mental processes that are relatively labile and of more recent evolutionary origin than in those parts of mental architecture which are that much older and more stable.

There may not be any good reason to dismiss the Whorfian position, but is there good reason to think that it is true? One indication to think that the structure of a language can shape the thoughts of its speakers comes from a study on the representation of stereotypes in Chinese–English bilinguals. The experimenters created a series of personality descriptions, some of which could be captured by a one-word label in English (such as *artistic* or *liberal*) but not Chinese, and some of which could be captured by a one-word label in Chinese but not English. The participants were then given a number of these descriptions to read in either English or Chinese, and five days later they were asked various questions about the personality types that they had read. Participants made more inferences about, and exhibited better recall for, the vignettes which included a one-word description than they did for the vignettes that did not include such a description. In other words, reading a description in one language rather than another seems to have an impact on the degree to which certain stereotypes are activated.

Further evidence of linguistic influence on thought comes from studies of mathematical cognition. One set of studies has explored the impact of a language's number vocabulary on the rate at which children acquire mathematical competency. It has been argued that English-speaking children have more difficulty learning to count between 10 and 20 than Chinese-speaking children do because the Chinese number words in this interval are more regular than the English terms are. (For example, the Chinese term for 11 is 'ten and one'.) Other studies have found that children who are bilingual in Welsh and English perform to a higher level when they calculate in English than when they calculate in Welsh, a finding that is perhaps explained by the fact that number words in Welsh are much longer than they are in English.

But perhaps the most profound impact of language on mathematical thought turns on the richness of a language's lexicon—its vocabulary. As we noted in the previous chapter, many non-human species can represent mathematical relations in approximate terms; thus, it is not surprising that this capacity is also present in societies with an impoverished mathematical vocabulary. What is more surprising is that the speakers of such languages appear to have little capacity to think about numerical relations in exact terms. Our evidence for this comes from studies of the Amazonian languages Pirahã and Mundurukú. Mundurukú has no terms for integers above 5, while Pirahã does not even appear to have terms for the numbers 1 or 2. This lack of number terms in these languages seems to be accompanied by a surprisingly poor grasp of mathematical relations. For example, Mundurukú speakers seem unable to tell whether subtracting 4 items from 6 items would leave one with 2 items, 1 item, or no items at all. Although the data here are still somewhat uncertain, this research provides some indication that the mastery of number words may be required for the capacity to reason about mathematic relations in exact terms.

Where does that leave us? Is human thought basically the same everywhere and at all times (as universalists claim), or does its nature vary in important respects from one cultural context to another (as particularists argue)?

The answer depends on the perspective that one adopts. The universalist account seems to be most plausible when we consider our basic cognitive capacities, such as the capacity to appreciate the logical relations between propositions or the capacity to group objects on the basis of their relations or shared membership in a common category. Although there is evidence of socially based variation in the modes of inference that individuals are most *likely* to employ, there is little evidence that the members of one society employ modes of inference that are beyond the comprehension of the members of another society.

On the other hand, there is little doubt that societies differ in the range of thoughts that are practically accessible to their members. As we have just noted, the presence of number words in a society can have a profound impact on the mathematical capacities of its members, but words are not the only tools that extend the reach of thought, for human thought is scaffolded in many ways. Thought is scaffolded by culturally transmitted practices, such as the habit of using one's fingers to enumerate the members of a set or the practice of remembering a list by imaginatively placing each of its members in a separate room of one's house. Thought is scaffolded by social institutions, such as schools, scientific communities, and publishing houses. And thought is scaffolded by artefacts of various kinds, such as the sextant, the slide rule, and the smartphone. Thus, even if the basic cognitive capacities of human beings are fundamentally unchanged from one setting to another, the thoughts that are readily available to the members of one society may differ in radical ways from those that are available to the members of another society, for the regions of cognitive space that are accessible to a person depend not only on their basic cognitive capacities but also on the ways in which those capacities are scaffolded, and the scaffolds of thought are not everywhere the same.

Chapter 6
Thought gone wrong

'How could you, a mathematician, believe that extraterrestrials were sending you messages?' 'Because the ideas I had about supernatural beings came to me the same way my mathematical ideas did,' came the answer.

Sylvia Nasar, *A Beautiful Mind*

As with any other bodily organ, the organs of thought are susceptible to breakdown and malfunction. Such impairments often result in delusions—pathologies of thought. Although delusions are relatively easy to identify, the class of delusions is not easily defined. The American Psychiatric Association characterizes a delusion as a 'false belief based on incorrect inference about external reality that is firmly sustained despite what everyone else believes and despite what constitutes incontrovertible or obvious proof or evidence to the contrary'. There is much that is problematic about this characterization— delusions need not be false, nor need they concern 'external reality'—but it does capture the essential feature of delusions: delusional thoughts have become 'disconnected from reality'.

Delusions provide the student of thought with much to puzzle over. What kinds of thoughts are delusions? How might delusions be explained? And what, if anything, might delusions be able to tell us about the architecture of thought? We will not be able to provide detailed answers to these questions in this chapter, but we will point to where some of the answers might lie.

The nature of delusions

Delusions can take various forms. Some delusional patients suffer from *monothematic delusions*, so-called because the patient's delusions are restricted to a single topic. Many monothematic delusions are characterized by their bizarre content. For example, the Capgras delusion is characterized by the thought that someone close to one (typically a family member) is an imposter rather than the person whom they claim to be. Cotard's delusion is characterized by the conviction that parts of one's body are rotting or—in extreme cases—by the thought that one is dead. Among the 'first rank' symptoms of schizophrenia is the delusion that one's actions are under the control of other agents (the delusion of alien control) and the delusion that thoughts are being inserted into one's mind by other agents (the delusion of thought insertion). Other monothematic delusions involve relatively mundane thoughts, such as the conviction that one's spouse is being unfaithful or that one is being persecuted by one's neighbours or the government. These thoughts qualify as delusions not because their content is fantastical—after all, spouses can be unfaithful and governments have been known to persecute their citizens—but because they are held with an intensity and conviction that are not commensurate with the evidence available to the individual.

Monothematic delusions can be contrasted with *polythematic delusions*, delusions that are not restricted to a single theme but encompass a broad array of topics. The story of the German high-court judge Daniel Schreber provides a classic example of a polythematic delusion. Schreber's web of delusional beliefs included the conviction that God was transforming him into a woman, transmitting rays down to enact miracles upon him, and sending little men to torture him. A more recent example of a polythematic delusion involves the Princeton mathematician John

Nash, whose network of delusional thoughts included the conviction that he was the Emperor of Antarctica and the left foot of God, that aliens were sending him encrypted messages through the *New York Times*, and that any man wearing a red necktie was a member of a secret international communist organization.

Delusions are thoughts, but what kind of thoughts are they? There are questions about both the content of delusions and their attitude. Let us begin with the question of content.

In some cases (e.g. delusions of paranoia) it is reasonably clear what the content of the delusion is. Someone who says that he is being hounded by government agents probably believes just what he says. But in other cases it is difficult to know what—if anything—the content of a delusion might be. Consider John Nash's claim to be the left foot of God. What precisely might such a claim mean? Is it a metaphor for something? If so, what? Or consider the claim of a patient who believed that her mother changed into another person every time she put her glasses on. Again, it is far from clear what precisely the content of the thought underlying such a claim could be. We may be able to attach *some* kind of sense to such claims, but they take us close to the limits of intelligibility. In some cases delusional utterances may be attempts to communicate a thought whose content is highly obscure, but in other cases delusional utterances may be empty speech acts behind which there is no underlying thought at all.

What about the attitude component of delusions? What kinds of thoughts are delusions? The standard answer is that delusions are beliefs. However, psychiatrists have long had reservations about the 'doxastic' conception of delusions. ('Doxastic' is derived from *doxa*, the Greek word for belief or opinion.) There are various respects in which the doxastic account is problematic, but perhaps the most serious objection to it is that delusions often fail to generate the kinds of behavioural and emotional responses that one would expect them to generate if they were beliefs. As the Swiss psychiatrist Eugen Bleuler noted, it is not uncommon for those with delusions to behave as if their delusional statements are to be understood 'only symbolically'. For example, a patient who claims to be Napoleon may be quite happy to be ordered to bed.

But if delusions are not beliefs, what might they be? It has sometimes been suggested that delusions are a kind of non-committal mental state. Perhaps the patient who claims to be Napoleon does not really believe that he is Napoleon, but is instead engaging in a kind of imaginative make-believe—he is merely *pretending* to be Napoleon. What should we make of this idea?

We should certainly allow that some delusions might *originate* in acts of make-believe. For example, an episode of delusional jealousy might begin with the 'mere thought' that one's spouse is having an affair. At this point, the patient might attach no credence to the idea—the possibility is merely entertained, as it were. But to say that a delusion might originate as a non-committal mental state is not to say that it will continue to retain that status, for once the thought has occurred to the individual it might lodge itself in their mind as a live possibility, and over time evolve into a robust conviction that is 'firmly sustained despite what everyone else believes'.

Certainly some delusions take on the nature of beliefs. Jules Cotard, the French psychiatrist who lent his name to the Cotard delusion, reported that one of his patients not only claimed to be dead but also lay down in a coffin and demanded to be buried. Similarly, Capgras patients have been known to behave aggressively towards a family member because they believed that the person in question was not who they claimed to be. Indeed, delusions can have fatal consequences. In one case a man developed the delusion that he had two heads, one of which he thought belonged to his late wife's gynecologist. The patient came to the attention of psychiatrists because he had been hospitalized for gunshot wounds as a result of a failed attempt to remove the 'second' head. If a person's actions provide any guide to their beliefs, then there seems little doubt that this patient really did believe that he had two heads.

Explaining delusions

Let us turn from the question of how delusions might be accommodated without our taxonomy of thoughts to the question of how delusions might be explained. Why might someone believe, in the face of all apparent evidence to the contrary, that their neighbours are persecuting them, that their wife has been replaced by an imposter, or that God is implanting thoughts into their head?

We can distinguish two kinds of explanations that one might provide for a thought. On the one hand, one might provide a brutely causal (or 'physiological') explanation for why someone has a particular thought. Applied to the case of delusions, one might explain the genesis of a delusion by appealing to the fact that the person has suffered a brain injury of a certain kind, or by pointing to the fact that they have abnormal levels of a certain neurotransmitter. Neuropsychiatry is starting to sketch explanations of this kind for certain types of delusions—for example, there is evidence that delusions are associated with damage to the right frontal lobe, and that some schizophrenic delusions may be associated with abnormal levels of dopamine—although we are still some way off from a complete causal understanding of delusions.

Purely causal explanations of a thought can be contrasted with 'rationalizing explanations'—explanations that make the acquisition of the thought intelligible from the agent's point of view. A rationalizing explanation would not merely explain what *caused* the relevant delusion but would provide a *reason* for it such that we could understand why the individual in question found that thought so compelling. Is it possible to provide a rationalizing account of delusions?

Influential voices in the history of psychiatry have suggested that the answer to this question might be 'no'. In his monumental *General Psychopathology*, the psychiatrist Karl Jaspers claimed that there is a profound difference between 'that type of psychic life that we can intuit and understand, and that type which, in its own way, is not understandable and which is truly distorted and schizophrenic'. There is good reason to take Jaspers's claim seriously. After all, it is not obvious that thought can always be made intelligible. Perhaps some thoughts can be explained only in purely causal or 'physiological' terms. Nonetheless, even if there is no guarantee that delusions can be provided with rationalizing explanations, we have every reason to look for such explanations. For one thing, a rationalizing explanation for delusions might provide a bridge between delusional and non-delusional forms of belief, such that we could describe delusional thought as lying on a continuum with 'ordinary' forms of thought rather than as something qualitatively distinct from it.

So, what might a rationalizing explanation of delusions look like? What kinds of psychological processes might explain why individuals form beliefs 'despite what constitutes incontrovertible or obvious proof or evidence to the contrary'?

One possibility is that certain delusions are grounded in motivational processes. We certainly know that motivational factors can have a profound influence on belief formation. They influence not only the kind of evidence that we look for, but also the way in which we evaluate the evidence that we have. We see the effects of such factors in the phenomenon of self-deception. Usually, however, most of us are able to keep our self-deceptive tendencies in check. Perhaps delusions—or at least certain types of delusions—arise when these checks are removed.

It is clear that motivational factors play a role in the formation of *some* delusions. Most obviously, motivational factors seem to be at work in erotomania, also known as de Clerambault's delusion, in which the patient is convinced that someone of higher social status is secretly in love with them. Rather less obviously, motivational factors may also play a role in accounting for delusions of persecution. The psychologist Richard Bentall and his collaborators have developed an influential motivationally based account of persecutory delusions, according to which the patient develops persecutory delusions in order to protect their self-conception from perceived threats. The background to this account involves a contrast between two ways in which an event can be explained. An *externalizing* explanation of an event appeals to the influence of external or situational factors. For example, one might explain why one was not offered a job by supposing that the interview process was unfair. An *internalizing* explanation, by contrast, involves an appeal to one's own attributes and characteristics. For example, one might explain why one was not offered the job by supposing that one was not qualified for it. How does this distinction relate to the explanation of persecutory delusions? The idea is this. When faced with the need to explain an event, someone with a vulnerable self-conception will be strongly inclined to adopt an externalizing explanation ('the fates conspired against me') and overlook internalizing explanations ('I wasn't good enough') that might threaten their already fragile self-esteem. When taken to an extreme, one can see how such a tendency might lead to the formation of persecutory delusions. This account qualifies as a rationalizing explanation not because it represents persecutory delusions as based on evidence, but because it sees them as grounded in a familiar and understandable psychological drive—the drive to protect one's self-conception from external threats.

Delusions of persecution can perhaps be provided with a rationalizing explanation of the kind just outlined, but there are many delusions for which motivational factors do not seem to be relevant. What other kinds of rationalizing explanations might we appeal to in explaining delusions?

The American psychiatrist Brendan Maher has suggested that delusions can be regarded as 'theories' that the subject constructs in order to impose order and meaning on certain kinds of anomalous experiences. In fact, there are two ways in which anomalous experiences might give rise to delusions. One experiential impetus to delusions involves what has been dubbed the 'delusional mood'. The psychiatrist Karl Jaspers described what he called 'primary delusions' as 'the vague crystallizations of blurred delusional experience and diffuse, perplexing self-references'. In some manifestations of the delusional mood the subject might experience an object—a table, a remark, the arrangement of flowers in a vase—as possessing a degree of personal significance that it does not have. In other manifestations of the delusional mood subjects may complain that they can no longer grasp the significance of things. They might say that they feel alienated from the world, or that they cannot understand the relationships between objects. These experiences—the contents of which patients often struggle to articulate—can give rise to polythematic delusions as the patient attempts to find some meaning in the face of experiential chaos.

Whereas polythematic delusions often appear to be grounded in a generic delusional mood, monothematic delusions may be grounded in specific kinds of experiential anomalies. The flagship example of this approach is an account of the Capgras delusion that we owe to the neuropsychologists Hayden Ellis and Andrew Young. Ellis and Young began with a well-established model of face processing, according to which the visual system uses two pathways to process information about faces, a 'semantic' pathway that generates information about the identity of the face in question, and an affective pathway which generates an emotional response—the so-called 'feeling of familiarity'—to familiar faces. Ellis and Young hypothesized that the Capgras delusion is caused by damage to the affective pathway. Although the patient is able to *recognize* the faces of family members, this recognition is not accompanied by the normal feeling of familiarity. In order to explain this anomaly, the patient forms the belief that the person they are looking at is not the family member whom they claim to be but is instead an imposter. This model has been confirmed by the finding that the physiological response to familiar faces in Capgras patients is abnormally reduced.

Another delusion for which there is a plausible experience-based account is the delusion of alien control, a delusion in which the patient believes that their actions are under the control of alien forces. The account in question, which has been developed by the psychologist Chris Frith and his colleagues, runs as follows. In the normal brain, self-generated movement involves the operation of a model that allows the motor system to predict the sensory consequences of one's own actions. For example, the system predicts what it will feel like when one moves one's hand. As a result of these predictions, the sensory consequences of one's own actions are attenuated, and the sensations that they generate are less intense than the sensations that are generated when one's hand is moved by someone or something else. (This explains why it is difficult to tickle oneself.) However, there is evidence that this model is impaired in individuals who suffer from delusions of alien control, for such individuals experience the sensations that result from their own actions as no less intense than the sensations that result from the actions of other individuals. (This account predicts that patients with delusions of alien control will be able to tickle themselves, which turns out to be the case.) How might all this explain delusions of alien control? Because the sensory consequences of the patient's own actions are not attenuated in the way that they would normally be, such actions feel like they are under the control of external forces. Little wonder, then, that patients form the belief that their actions *are* under the control of other agents, for this belief seems to make some kind of sense of their bizarre and deeply disturbing experiences.

From experience to belief

Anomalous experiences appear to play an important role in the formation of a number of delusions, but there is reason to think that a full explanation of delusions must go beyond experiential anomalies. For one thing, there are many delusions—such as the belief that one is the left foot of God—that do not appear to be grounded in unusual experiences of any kind. Furthermore, even when a delusion *is* grounded in an unusual experience, there is invariably a gap of some kind between the content of the experience and the content of the resulting delusion: it is one thing to have experiences of unfamiliarity when looking at one's wife, and it is quite another to believe that one's wife has been replaced by an imposter. We need to explain why patients explain their anomalous experiences in the ways that they do ('My wife is an imposter') and reject the apparently more plausible explanations provided by friends, family and medical staff ('You have suffered a stroke that has damaged your visual system'). What kinds of non-experiential factors might contribute to the explanation of delusions?

Here is one idea that has been mooted as a possible factor. Consider a situation in which one's sensory evidence conflicts with one's background beliefs. For example, one might believe that all ducks can swim, only to be confronted with what appears to be a duck that is incapable of swimming. What should one do? Should one give up the belief that all ducks can swim or should one conclude that one's senses are deceiving one (as they sometimes do), and hold that although the animal in question looks like it duck, it is not a duck? There is no general strategy that one ought to adopt in reconciling sensory evidence with background belief. In some situations one should accept the testimony of one's senses and revise one's prior beliefs, in other situations one should retain one's background beliefs and conclude that one's senses are deceiving one, and in still other situations it might be appropriate to withhold judgement until one has further information (see page 17).

How might this issue bear on the explanation of delusions? Tony Stone and Andrew Young have suggested that delusional patients might have a general bias towards privileging 'observational evidence' at the expensive of background belief. Whereas a non-delusional person might conclude that their senses are deceiving them when faced with anomalous experiences of the kind that the delusional person has, the person with delusions tends to take their experiences at face value, and is more ready to revise their background beliefs than a non-delusional person would be.

Another candidate factor involves what has been called a 'jumping-to-conclusions' bias in belief-formation. In certain studies of belief-formation participants are presented with two jars, A and B, each of which contains coloured beads in a certain ratio. For example, jar A might contain seven red beads for every two blue beads, whereas these ratios might be reversed in jar B. Participants are then shown the beads that are supposedly being drawn from the jar (the selection of which is actually determined by the experimenters), and are instructed to guess which jar the beads are being drawn from. Studies have found that delusional individuals typically guess more quickly and are more certain of their guesses than non-delusional individuals are. In other words, delusional individuals seem to 'jump to conclusions': they appear to be willing to accept a hypothesis on the basis of less evidence than non-delusional subjects typically require.

Neither of these proposed 'second factors' is unproblematic. If delusional individuals have a general bias in favour of privileging observational evidence over background belief then one would expect them to be routinely taken in by perceptual illusions, and there is no evidence that this is the case. And if delusions are to be explained by a jumping-to-conclusions bias, why do delusional patients not jump from delusional belief to non-delusional belief when presented with evidence against the delusion? At the very least, the jumping-to-conclusions proposal will need to be

supplemented with an account of 'delusional fixity'—the fact that
delusions are often highly resistant to counter-evidence—if it is to
be at all plausible.

Perhaps it is no surprise that finding a plausible 'second factor'
has proven to be so challenging, for the very terms in which the
problem is posed provide little room for manoeuvre. Let me
explain. On the one hand, the sought-for second factor must
characterize belief-formation in general (rather than apply only
to selected domains of belief), for belief-formation is by its
very nature a holistic enterprise. But if the second factor were
domain-general, then one would expect its effects to be manifest
throughout the patient's entire body of beliefs; in other words, one
would expect the patient to have delusions about all manner of
topics. Monothematic delusions, however, are by definition
restricted to a particular topic: unlike the beliefs of patients with
polythematic delusions, the beliefs of patients with monothematic
delusions are in general unremarkable. In this respect, then, the
challenges we face in providing a rationalizing explanation of
monothematic delusions may be more acute than those posed by
polythematic delusions.

Learning from delusions

What might the study of delusions teach us about the nature of
thought in general? One lesson to emerge from the foregoing
concerns the challenge of accommodating delusions within our
ordinary 'folk psychological' conception of thought. As we noted,
legitimate questions can be raised about both the attitude and the
content of delusions. The worry here is not just that of identifying
what the content of a delusion is, or what kind of attitude the
person has to that content. The worry, rather, is that there may be
no fact of the matter about precisely what attitude or content
characterizes certain delusions. But our folk-psychological
conception of thought—which is the only conception of thought
that we have—requires that a thought have a determinate content

and attitude. It is possible that this framework will have to be fundamentally modified in order to accommodate certain delusions.

A second lesson to be drawn concerns the challenge posed by explaining delusions. Although motivational and experiential factors appear to play a role in the formation of certain types of delusion, we are still a long way from having a complete account of the genesis of delusions. In large part our problem stems from the fact that we lack a good model of *non-pathological* belief formation. We know that belief-formation involves interaction between background knowledge of the world and perceptual input, but we know very little about the nature of this interaction. For example, we do not know whether the processes that are implicated in it are domain-general or domain-specific, nor do we know how such processes balance the need to make sense of perceptual data against the need to take background considerations into account. Because we know so little about normal belief-formation, we have little idea of the ways in which it is possible for it to go wrong.

Let me close this chapter with one final reflection. When asked about the basis of his delusional thoughts, John Nash replied that he took his delusional ideas seriously because they 'came to me the same way my mathematical ideas did'. The idea that delusions are accompanied by a sense of intuitive obviousness is frequently encountered in the writings of those who suffer from them. Such claims have profound implications for understanding the relationship between thought and emotion. Some thoughts might be grounded in nothing more than a certain kind of emotional identification: the thought 'feels right'. It is as though sub-personal mechanisms track the plausibility of various ideas, attaching emotionally charged tags that read 'Endorse me' to some thoughts and 'Reject me' to others. We have conscious access to the tags that result from this process, but little idea why particular thoughts are given the tags that they are. Perhaps what happens in delusions is that this labelling process becomes derailed, and ideas that ought not be endorsed—'I am the Emperor of Antarctica'— are given the same tag of endorsement that accompanies profound mathematical insights. From the subject's point of view the thought simply 'feels right', and the suggestion that one should submit it to critical scrutiny might appear utterly absurd.

Chapter 7
The ethics of thought

> Many people would sooner die than think; in fact, they do so.
>
> Bertrand Russell

Some of what we do falls within the domain of what we are accountable for. We praise people for their acts of selfless generosity, and we blame them for their insensitivity to the needs of others. Other activities associated with a person fall outside the domain of that for which it is reasonable to hold them accountable. We do not praise those with the ability to sleep well, nor do we blame those with poor digestion. Where does thought fit into this picture? Is it reasonable to hold an individual responsible for their thoughts, or is thinking akin to sleeping and digesting—an activity for which we bear no responsibility?

It is clear that not all episodes of thought fall within the realm of moral responsibility. Someone who is undergoing a psychotic episode and who regards the doctors as enemy soldiers in disguise is not responsible for their thoughts. The question is not whether we are always responsible for our thoughts, but whether we are ever responsible for our thoughts. If we do possess some degree of responsibility for our thoughts, then there are further questions about the conditions under which we have such responsibility, and the ways in which we ought to exercise that responsibility. As we will see, addressing these questions will lead us into a maze of obscure and difficult issues that lie at the heart of the nature of thought.

Thought control

Let us begin with the statement by Bertrand Russell that functions as the epigraph for this chapter: 'Many people would sooner die than think; in fact, they do so.' The significance of Russell's statement turns on a distinction between two kinds of thought. As we noted in the first chapter, sometimes thought is passive. Just as one might find oneself in a feverish state, so too one might simply find oneself struck by the thought that life is fleeting or that one has lost one's keys. Russell's concern is not with thought in this sense, but with thought understood as an activity over which one has some degree of control. In other words, Russell's interest is with *thinking*. But just how much control do we have over thinking?

Thinking can be controlled in different ways. In some contexts the evolution of one's thoughts is controlled by the application of a rule or a recipe. For example, consider what is involved in counting backwards from 100 in multiples of 3. We have a recipe for counting backwards from 100, and executing this task requires keeping oneself on track, avoiding distractions, and applying the recipe in question. But counting backwards from 100 is in many ways an unusual kind of activity, and most episodes of controlled thinking involve no such recipe. Suppose that I ask you why democracies tend not to wage war against other democracies. If you have not already considered this question, you may need to think about it. What precisely does that involve? Well, if your experience is anything like mine, you put the question to yourself and wait for something to come to mind. Sometimes nothing much comes to mind and the question sits there unanswered; on other occasions, one's unconscious comes up with something intelligible. Either way, there is no algorithm or recipe that one can consciously follow in order to generate the required thoughts.

On the whole, thinking does not seem to extend much beyond putting questions to oneself and waiting for the unconscious to get around to answering them. The role of consciousness in such cases seems to be restricted to that of a minder charged with ensuring that one's mind does not wander off topic. We are, however, surprisingly poor at keep our mind-wandering tendencies in check, as the psychologist Jonathan Schooler has documented. In one study, Schooler asked people to read a passage to themselves, and to monitor themselves for periods during which they were 'zoning out'. Participants were then probed at random intervals to see whether their mind had wandered or whether they were still reading the passage as instructed. Schooler discovered that subjects had often zoned out whilst they were meant to be reading, and—even more surprisingly—that they often had not realized (until probed) that they had been zoning out!

Not only are we poor at keeping ourselves focused on a particular task, there is evidence that the very attempt to control the direction of one's stream of thought can backfire. In a famous study, the psychologist Daniel Wegner and his colleagues asked participants *not* to think about white bears during a five-minute period. They found that those participants who had received this instruction reported more white-bear thoughts than did participants who had been specifically instructed to think about white bears. In other words, the very attempt to suppress a thought can be counterproductive. Wegner dubbed this phenomenon the 'ironic control of thought'. Investigation into the ironic control of thought has obvious relevance to various pathologies of thought, such as obsessive–compulsive disorder. So, although we have some conscious control over the direction of our thoughts, such control as we possess is far from unlimited. And to the extent that we have relatively little control over the direction of our thoughts, perhaps we also have relatively little responsibility for what we think.

Doxastic voluntarism

Let us turn from the question of what kind of control we possess over our thoughts in general to the more specific question of what kind of control we possess over our *beliefs*. Advocates of a position known as 'doxastic voluntarism' claim that we have some degree of direct control over the formation of our beliefs. ('Doxastic' is derived from 'doxa', the Greek term for belief.) Few doxastic voluntarists claim that a person's control over their beliefs is *unlimited*—that would be a pretty implausible view, for it is fairly obvious that one cannot decide to believe just anything. (The Queen in Lewis Carroll's *Through the Looking Glass* might have been able to believe six impossible things before breakfast, but that is a feat that few of us can match.) Rather, doxastic voluntarists claim only that we have some degree of control over whether or not to accept those propositions that are 'open questions' for us—propositions whose truth or falsity is not settled by our evidence.

One reason to take doxastic voluntarism seriously concerns an apparent contrast between perception and belief. Although one has some degree of control over where to look, given that one is looking at a certain object one has little control over what it is that one sees. Perception is in this sense passive—it is something that happens to one. By contrast, thought does not seem to be passive in quite the same way. To use a Kantian term, thought seems to be 'spontaneous'. Consider a situation in which a close friend has been accused of a crime. The evidence against the friend is not overwhelming but it is significant. At the same time, the friend claims that she is innocent, and one's knowledge of her character inclines one to think that she is telling the truth. In such cases, are we not tempted to describe ourselves as 'making up our mind' about what to believe?

Perhaps so, but these matters are murky. We may be tempted to use the language of decision in these contexts, but belief-formation is rarely (if ever) accompanied by the experience of choice. Does it seem as though one decides whether or not to believe in the innocence of one's friend? Not to me at any rate. Instead, it seems to me that one simply *finds oneself* with a certain view of the matter. Perhaps one finds oneself convinced by the evidence against her, or perhaps one finds oneself convinced that she must be telling the truth. Or perhaps one is not sure what to believe. But whichever of these possibilities obtains, belief formation does not seem to involve an act of the will in the way in which raising one's arm or opening one's eyes does.

A further mark against doxastic voluntarism is that the kinds of incentives that normally apply to decision-making do not seem to have any grip over the formation of belief. I can motivate you to attend the play that I have written by giving you a free ticket, but I cannot in the same way motivate you to believe that the play is a good one. This is not to deny that motivational factors can influence belief formation, but such factors are effective only when concealed from the gaze of consciousness—they do not function in the direct way in which financial incentives do. The kind of reasons that turn the 'handle of belief' are not prudential reasons that concern what one might gain from forming the relevant belief but evidential reasons that concern whether or not it is true.

Although belief-formation may not be under our direct control, we do possess various forms of indirect control over what we believe. For example, we can critically evaluate those ideas that are presented to us as potential candidates for belief. We can take a step back from claims that seem plausible and ask whether the evidence in their favour is as strong as it appears to be. We can probe new aspects of our environment, and thus acquire beliefs about topics of which we had been ignorant. Perception provides a simple example of this capacity. The perceptual interrogation of an object—for example, looking at it or sniffing it—brings one's belief-forming mechanisms under its effective control. Much the same happens when one reads a newspaper, although in this case the beliefs in question are not primarily about what one sees but concern the subject of the newspaper report. By choosing to expose oneself to certain kinds of information rather than others one exerts a kind of indirect control over the contours of one's conception of the world.

Truth or consequences?

The appropriateness of the kind of doxastic control that we have just examined is uncontroversial, but there are forms of doxastic control that are rather more problematic. Consider Blaise Pascal's famous wager argument for belief in the existence of God. Pascal argued that one should believe that God exists whether or not one has evidence for the existence of God, for—roughly speaking—a cost-benefit of analysis of the consequences of belief reveals that one is better off believing that God exists than one is by failing to believe that God exists, whether or not God does in fact exist. We are not concerned here with the details of Pascal's argument, or indeed with his account of how one might install belief in oneself in the absence of evidence, but with the question of whether there is something morally problematic about the course of action that Pascal recommends. Is there something wrong—or at least 'inauthentic'—with attempting to believe a proposition that one takes to lack evidential support?

The Victorian philosopher William Clifford certainly thought so. In his essay 'The Ethics of Belief', Clifford argued that legitimate belief-formation is governed by a requirement of sufficient evidence. Clifford opened his essay with the tale of a shipowner who formed the 'sincere and comfortable conviction' that his ship was safe despite good evidence to the contrary. The ship sank, and all those on board perished. Clifford claimed that the owner was guilty of their deaths, for he had no right to believe that the ship was safe. Clifford drew a general moral from this tale: it is, he claimed, wrong 'everywhere, always, and for anyone, to believe anything upon insufficient evidence'.

There is something intuitively attractive about 'Clifford's dictum', as it has come to be called. As the story of the negligent shipowner demonstrates, beliefs have consequences, and false beliefs can have disastrous consequences. Had Clifford been writing a century later than he did, he may well have told a tale about the consequences that flow from belief in the superiority of one's ethnic group, religious community, or political party. But despite its *prima facie* plausibility, there is much that is puzzling about Clifford's dictum. What is 'sufficient evidence'? What sort of obligations do we have to collect 'sufficient evidence'? And why exactly might it be wrong to believe something on the basis of insufficient evidence?

Clifford never gave an analysis of 'sufficient evidence', and perhaps there is good reason for that: it is a very difficult thing to do. In the absence of an agreed analysis of the notion, let us equate 'sufficient evidence' with the kind of evidence that would convince a jury of reasonable and impartial persons. How plausible is Clifford's dictum if 'reasonable evidence' is understood in this way?

Rather implausible, it seems. As the American philosopher Peter van Inwagen has pointed out, accepting this version of Clifford's dictum would call into question a great many of our beliefs. Few religious beliefs, for example, are supported by the kind of evidence that would convince a jury of reasonable and impartial observers. Of course, the advocate of Clifford's dictum might think that religious beliefs are precisely the kinds of beliefs that we ought not hold—indeed, religious belief was the central target of Clifford's own essay—but the problematic consequences of Clifford's dictum go far beyond the realm of religion. Endorsing Clifford's dictum threatens to undermine our right to hold many of our most cherished beliefs about morality, politics, and philosophy, for these are domains in which it is notoriously difficult to secure consensus, even among reasonable and impartial persons. Indeed, there are a great many scientific issues about which there is no such consensus.

One reason why it is often difficult to secure consensus even between reasonable and impartial persons is that the degree to which a person finds a particular proposal plausible depends on their background beliefs. A claim that might be very plausible given one set of background beliefs might be highly implausible when evaluated in light of a different set of background beliefs. And of course even reasonable and impartial jurors may differ in their background beliefs. Do the demands of rationality require that one have sufficient evidence not just for the particular claim under consideration but also for all of one's background beliefs? That requirement would surely be too demanding, for it is doubtful whether we can comply with it. Indeed, it is not even clear what it would mean to subject all of one's beliefs to critical scrutiny 'as a whole'. Arguably, one can subject a claim to critical scrutiny only in light of the rest of one's body of beliefs.

We have seen that Clifford's dictum faces serious objections, but perhaps there is something to it nonetheless. What might be said in defence Clifford's dictum?

One argument for Clifford's dictum begins with the thought that the less evidence there is in favour of a belief, the more likely it is to be false. Although this claim is not uncontroversial, let us accept it for the sake of argument. The question is whether belief-formation should be governed solely by a concern with truth. What is so great about truth anyway?

One of the advantages of truth is instrumental. In general, acting on true (or at least close-to-true) beliefs is more likely to secure one's goals than acting on false beliefs is. Of course, having false beliefs can *sometimes* be to one's advantage—consider the lucky traveller who missed their flight because they went to the wrong gate, only to discover that the flight ended in tragedy—but such cases are exceptions to the general rule linking truth to success. Creatures like us that inhabit complex and rapidly changing environments have particularly strong reasons to form true beliefs, for we never know when a certain piece of information might bear on the success of a future project.

But although there is much to be said for the view that a creature with belief-forming mechanisms that track the truth will generally be better off than a creature whose belief-forming mechanisms do not track the truth, there may be domains in which a decent dose of self-deception is to one's advantage. Perhaps those of us who have an overly rosy self-conception are better off than those of us who have an accurate self-conception. Certainly there is ample evidence that human beings *do* in general have an overly positive view of themselves. Most drivers believe that they are better-than-average drivers; most teachers believe that they are better-than-average teachers; and most people believe that they have a less biased self-conception than other people do! In fact, having an overly positive self-image may even be a universal trait. Rather than assuming that natural selection always privileges the formation of true belief over its alternatives, there may be domains in which self-serving biases in belief-formation have been selected for.

The possibility for conflict between truth and consequences is not limited to an individual's view of themselves but extends to matters of social and political importance. Consider the possibility that scientific developments might undermine belief in (say) the reality of free will or the objectivity of morality. Whether or not science will undermine such beliefs, it is widely thought that it *could*. But one might also think that giving up on belief in free will or the objectivity of morality has the potential to undermine many of the social and political institutions that are central to our identity as human beings. And if that is right, then the directive to believe only what is true—or, more carefully, to believe only what one's evidence supports—might undermine the conditions that are required for human flourishing. At this point it is no longer so obvious that we ought to side with truth when forced to choose between it and consequences.

Of course, one might argue that whatever the instrumental value of true belief, it also has an intrinsic value. Perhaps true belief is like love, friendship, and beauty—something that is a good in and of itself. I think there is something to this thought, at least where it concerns beliefs about matters of consequence. (There does not seem to be anything intrinsically valuable about having true beliefs about trivial issues, such as how many knives and forks there are in the cutlery drawer.) But even if true belief about important matters *is* of intrinsic value, it does not follow that the value of truth should always trump every other value with which it might compete.

Chapter 8
The limits of thought

> Our intellect holds the same position in the world of thought
> as our body occupies in the expanse of nature.
>
> Pascal, *Pensées*

Although there are places on the surface of Earth—not to mention its interior—that are untouched by human exploration, we have done a reasonably thorough job of exploring our own backyard. The same, however, cannot be said of the real estate beyond our planet, for as a species we have barely left home. No doubt the human exploration of our galaxy will continue apace, but even on the most optimistic of estimates we are likely to visit only a fraction of the universe, for given our physical limitations vast tracts of space and time are simply inaccessible to us.

The scope of human exploration might be limited, but what about the scope of human thought? Is thought also restricted in its range, or are there no limits on what we can grasp in thought? Although the issue is not beyond controversy, we can take it for granted that there are truths for which we may never have any evidence. The deeper question on which we will focus in this chapter is whether there are thoughts that we cannot even entertain. In other words, are there aspects of reality from which we are *cognitively closed*?

The idea that certain aspects of reality might be beyond our grasp might at first seem implausible. After all, one point of contrast between perception and thought is that thought is not limited in the way that perception is. As we noted in Chapter 1, although certain features of the world might be too small for us to see, too subtle for us to smell, or too far away for us to touch, on the face of things there does not seem to be any aspect of the world that we cannot think about. Is there any reason to take the possibility of cognitive closure seriously?

There is. Given that the machinery of human thought is part of our biological inheritance, there is every reason to expect that it suffers from the kinds of bugs and blindspots that constrain other biological systems. Without wishing to detract from their remarkable capacities, it is doubtful whether chimpanzees possess the ability to think about quantum mechanics or whether scrub jays can grasp the fundamentals of geometry. But if there are regions of reality that are inaccessible to the grasp of other species, why should we assume that no region of reality is inaccessible to our grasp? We might be *less* subject to cognitive closure than any other species, but surely it would be the height of hubris to assume that the light of human reason can illuminate every corner of the cosmos.

It is one thing to grant that we are subject to cognitive closure, but it is quite another to identify precisely which aspects of reality lie beyond our grasp. Is it possible to demarcate the borders of human thought? The question might seem absurd. After all, one might argue that if a certain thought really is unthinkable then we could not be in a position to think about it, let alone know that it was unthinkable. But in fact there is nothing paradoxical about attempting to determine where the limits of thought lie. The key to appreciating this fact involves distinguishing thinking about a thought from actually thinking it. Suppose I think to myself, 'Nishat's thought is making her happy.' In this case, I have thought about Nishat's thought without actually thinking it. So too, the task of providing an abstract specification of the limits of thought need not require one to think the unthinkable. Just as one might be able to know what it is that one does not know (the 'known unknowns'), so too one might be able to think about what it is that one cannot think (the 'thinkable unthinkables').

Let us now consider three aspects of reality which many theorists have claimed to lie beyond our powers of comprehension: the nature of consciousness, the nature of things in themselves, and the nature of God.

Consciousness

If you are anything like me you may enjoy a strong cup of coffee while you read. Let us suppose that you are enjoying such a cup right now, and that you have the familiar experience of the taste of coffee. What is the relationship between your current brain state and your conscious experience of the coffee? Why is this brain state associated with consciousness, and why is it associated with this particular kind of conscious experience (the taste of coffee) rather than some other kind of conscious experience (such as the smell of sardines or the sound of a cello playing middle C)?

Despite many centuries of thought, no one has yet provided answers to these questions that have any plausibility. The problem is not that there are various accounts of the relationship between the brain and consciousness on the market and that current evidence fails to favour one account over another. Rather, the problem is that no one has yet offered an account that could *possibly* explain how conscious experience emerges from neural activity. In the words of the American philosopher Joseph Levine, there seems to be an *explanatory gap* between states of the brain and states of consciousness.

Some theorists argue that our ignorance in this regard is merely temporary, and that advances in neuroscience will bring with them

Thought

concepts that can bridge the gap between neural activity and conscious experience. Other theorists—often known as 'mysterians'—argue that our ignorance here is irremediable, and that we are constitutionally incapable of grasping the relationship between the brain and consciousness. The 19th-century English physicist John Tyndall expressed precisely this view when he wrote:

> The passage from the physics of the brain to the corresponding facts of consciousness is unthinkable. Granted that a definite thought, and a definite molecular action in the brain occur simultaneously; we do not possess the intellectual organ, nor apparently any rudiment of the organ, which would enable us to pass, by a process of reasoning, from the one to the other.

There are various arguments for mysterianism, some of which are more plausible than others. One argument appeals to the fact that despite many centuries of reflection on the topic we have thus far been unable to come up with any remotely plausible account of the explanatory nexus between brain states and conscious states. This line of argument is far from overwhelming. After all, perhaps we are in roughly the same position vis-à-vis consciousness that mathematicians were in before they discovered zero or physicists were in before they recognized the distinction between velocity and acceleration. Perhaps all it takes is for someone to have a *really good idea*, and an understanding of the relationship between consciousness and the brain will be within our grasp.

A more promising argument for mysterianism has been developed by the philosopher Colin McGinn, who argues that the relationship between consciousness and the brain is beyond our grasp because of constraints on the acquisition of concepts. According to McGinn, our only source of information about consciousness is via introspection and our only source of information about the brain is via perception. Thus, we have no information channel that provides us with access to both consciousness and the brain, and we can never form the concepts that are required for understanding how consciousness emerges from neural activity. There *is* such an account, but—McGinn holds—it lies beyond the limits of our thought.

McGinn's argument has not gone unchallenged. Perhaps its most controversial assumption is that our ability to develop concepts is directly constrained by the information channels that we have. Critics point to the natural sciences as proof that the human mind is able to forge concepts that outrun the sensory information that is available to it. Perhaps, they continue, we will also be able to develop concepts that do justice to the explanatory nexus between physical states and experiential states, even though such concepts are not directly grounded in either introspection or perception. The challenge of mysterianism is an important one, but it would be premature to conclude that understanding how consciousness emerges from neural activity exceeds our powers of comprehension.

Things in themselves

An important philosophical tradition holds that our knowledge of the world is necessarily restricted to the ways in which things appear to us, and that we can never grasp the nature of things as they are in themselves. This doctrine is most famously associated with the German philosopher Immanuel Kant, who distinguished things as they appear to us (the phenomena) from things as they are in themselves (the noumena). According to Kant, science is limited to the realm of appearances, and it can never provide us with access to what underlies those appearances.

The interpretation of Kant's ideas is a notoriously contested topic, and here is not the place to enter into a discussion of precisely what he meant. Instead, I will focus on just one version of Kant's argument for the unknowability of things in themselves, an account that has been developed in most detail by the philosopher Rae Langton.

On Langton's reading, Kant's position revolves around a distinction between two types of properties—intrinsic properties and relational properties. An object's intrinsic properties are the properties that it possesses in and of itself, independently of the existence of other objects. An object's relational properties, as the name suggests, are the properties that it possesses in virtue of its relations to other objects. (For example, 'being married' is a relational property.) According to Langton, when Kant claims that we cannot have any insight into things as they are in themselves he means that we cannot have any insight into the intrinsic nature of objects.

Kant's argument for this position, Langton suggests, turns on a claim about the causal powers of objects. A causal power of an object is the power that it has to modify or affect the objects around it in some way. For example, a bell's causal powers include the capacity to produce distinctive kinds of sound waves. Now, Kant argues that an object's causal powers are not intrinsic to it but feature among its relational properties. If that is right, then we cannot have any access to its intrinsic properties, for our only access to the nature of an object is via its causal powers. The interrogation of nature involves 'poking' and 'prodding' things and then looking to see what effects this has on us. We have no other method for doing science. As Kant puts it:

The limits of thought

> The receptivity of our mind, its power of receiving representations in so far as it is affected in any way, is called 'sensibility'...Our nature is such that our intuition can never be other than sensible, that is, it contains only the way in which we are affected by objects.

So, if knowledge of things is restricted to understanding their causal powers, and if the causal powers of things are not among their intrinsic properties, then we can have no knowledge of intrinsic properties. Indeed, the outlook is actually even worse than this: not only can we never *know* what an object's intrinsic properties are, we cannot even *think* about such properties in any substantive fashion. This position—which Langton dubs 'Kantian humility'—is of course a form of cognitive closure.

One response to Kantian humility is to reject the claim that the way an object affects other objects depends only on its relational properties. In fact, perhaps most contemporary philosophers would make precisely this move, arguing that an object's tendency to behave in a certain way when (say) subjected to sound waves is a function of its intrinsic nature in conjunction with whatever laws of nature are operative in the relevant context. But, Langton argues, this position fares no better when it comes to providing us with insight into the nature of things as they are in themselves, for if (as seems plausible) the intrinsic nature of an object is only contingently connected to its causal powers, then it may not be possible to reason back from an object's causal powers to its intrinsic nature. In other words, it may turn out that the intrinsic nature of the world is beyond the reach of our thought whether or not a object's causal powers are merely relational.

God

A third domain in which claims of cognitive closure have been defended concerns the nature of God. Many religions harbour a mystical tradition in which God is said to elude the grasp of human thought. As the German scholar of religion Rudolf Otto put it, the nature of God is said to be something that man can 'neither proclaim in speech nor conceive in thought'. This approach to theology is often referred to as the *via negativa*, for its advocates hold that we can grasp only those properties that God lacks.

Some theologians argue that we cannot form a positive conception of God because God *has* no positive nature. To put this view paradoxically, our inability to grasp the nature of God is grounded in a feature of God's nature—namely, that God has no nature. Although this line of thought is not unpopular, it is of dubious coherence. After all, is it really possible that something could lack a nature? Must not everything that exists at least possess the property of existing? And must it not also have the property of being self-identical? And what about so-called negative properties, such as the property of *not* being a prime number or the property of *not* being a Bolivian citizen? Should not the advocate of the *via negativa* grant that God possesses these properties? And if such a person should object that these properties are not 'real properties'—and perhaps they are not—then must they not at least grant that God has some real ('positive') properties in virtue of which God is not a prime number or a citizen of Bolivia?

A more powerful motivation for the *via negativa* appeals to features on our side of the equation to explain our inability to grasp the nature of God. Again, the primary rationale for this claim involves an appeal to the processes that underlie the acquisition of concepts. We cannot latch on to God's nature by a process of abstraction from our acquaintance with the world of mundane reality, for there is—so the mystic claims—an unbridgeable gulf between God's attributes and those of the terrestrial objects with which we are familiar.

Could the nature of God be completely beyond our ability to grasp? The critic might point out that in describing God as ineffable the mystic has applied at least one property to God— namely, the property of being incomprehensible. But if God has that property, then it follows that God has at least one property that we can grasp, and thus that God's nature is not completely beyond us.

The mystic need not be bowed by this objection. They could say that although the claim 'God is ineffable' looks like it predicates a property of God, that appearance is deceptive. Just as the sentence

'Unicorns are non-existent' appears to predicate a property of unicorns (namely, the property of non-existence), in fact it does nothing of the sort. Instead, such a claim is more perspicuously rendered as 'It is not the case that unicorns exist.' Alternatively, the mystic could grant that incomprehensibility is a property, but insist that in ascribing this property to God one is in no way flouting the central tenets of the *via negativa*, for incomprehensibility is a merely *relational* property. One can know that God is incomprehensible without having any insight into God's intrinsic nature.

Concluding thoughts

We have examined three domains in which claims about cognitive closure have been advanced. As we have seen, some degree of controversy surrounds each of these claims, but taken together the arguments that accompany these claims go a long way towards motivating epistemic humility. Our powers of thought may be vastly superior to those of our fellow creatures, but they are very unlikely to be absolutely unlimited.

But wherever the boundaries of human thought might lie, there is no doubt whatsoever that we are very far from having reached them. There are thoughts—deep, important, and profound thoughts—that no human being has entertained. I opened this volume with a quotation from Blaise Pascal, so perhaps it is appropriate to conclude with another quotation from Pascal:

> All our dignity, then, consists in thought. By it we must elevate ourselves, and not by space and time which we cannot fill. Let us endeavour, then, to think well; this is the principle of morality.

References

Chapter 1: What is thought?

René Descartes's description of thought as a 'universal instrument which can be used in all kinds of situations' can be found in his *Discourse on Method and Related Writings* (1637).

The quotation from David Hume is taken from a chapter entitled 'Of the Association of Ideas', which can be found in his book *An Enquiry Concerning Human Understanding* (1748).

The classic paper in the study of reasoning that introduced the Wason selection task is Peter Wason 'Reasoning', in B.M. Foss (ed.) *New Horizons in Psychology* (London: Penguin, 1966).

The point that logic does not dictate what to believe can be found in Gilbert Harman's book *Change in View* (Cambridge, MA: MIT Press, 1988).

Chapter 2: The mechanical mind

Haugeland's claim that 'If you take care of the syntax, the semantics will take care of itself' is to be found in his 'Semantic engines: An introduction to mind design', in J. Haugeland (ed.) *Mind Design* (Cambridge, MA: MIT Press, 1981).

John Searle's Chinese room argument can be found in his paper 'Minds, Brains, and Programs', first published in the journal *Behavioral and Brain Sciences* (1980) and reprinted many times since.

The quotation from Ludwig Wittgenstein used in the final section of the chapter appears in his book *Zettel*.

Chapter 3: The inner sanctum

Wittgenstein's beetle-in-the-box analogy can be found in his *Philosophical Investigations* (§293).

Details of the brain-decoding study can be found in J.D. Haynes et al. (2007) 'Reading hidden intentions in the human brain', *Current Biology*, 17: 323–8.

Details of the neuroimaging study of the vegetative state patient can be found in A.M. Owen et al. (2006) 'Detecting awareness in the vegetative state', *Science*, 313: 1402.

Chapter 4: Brute thought

The study of mathematical cognition in rats can be found in Church, R.M. and Meek, W.H. (1984) 'The numerical attribute of stimuli', in H.L. Roitblat, T. Bever and H.S. Terrace (eds) *Animal Cognition* (Hillsdale, NJ: Erlbaum), pp. 445–64.

Details of the chocolate chip study can be found in D.M. Rumbaugh et al. (1987) 'Summation in the chimpanzee (*Pan troglodytes*)', *Journal of Experimental Psychology: Animal Behavior Processes*, 13: 107–15.

The anecdote regarding Sheba and Sarah is taken from S.T. Boysen et al (1996) 'Quantity-based inference and symbolic representation in chimpanzees (Pan troglodytes)', *Journal of Experimental Psychology: Animal Behavior Processes*, 22: 76–86.

The study involving chimpanzees trained to use plastic tags to represent the relations of sameness and difference can be found in R.K.R. Thompson et al. (1997) 'Language-naïve chimpanzees (Pan troglodytes) judge relations between relations in a conceptual matching-to-sample task,' *Journal of Experimental Psychology: Animal Behavior Processes*, 23: 31–43.

Details of social reasoning in baboons can be found in D. Cheney and R. Seyfarth *Baboon Metaphysics* (Chicago: Chicago University Press, 2007).

Details about the Povinelli and Eddy study can be found in Povinelli, D. and Eddy, T.J. (1996) 'What young chimpanzees know about seeing', *Monographs of the Society for Research in Child Development*, 61: 1–152.

Details about the study by Brian Hare and colleagues can be found in B. Hare et al. (2002) 'Chimpanzees know what conspecifics do and do not see', *Animal Behaviour*, 59: 771–85.

A review of David Smith's work on metacognition and uncertainty monitoring can be found in J. Smith et al. (2003) 'The comparative psychology of uncertainty monitoring and meta-cognition', *Behavioral and Brain Sciences*, 26: 317–73.

Derek Browne discusses the evidence of metacognition in dolphins in his paper (2004) 'Do dolphins know their own minds?', *Biology and Philosophy*, 19: 633–53.

The quotation from Andy Clark is taken from his paper (2006) 'Material symbols', *Philosophical Psychology*, 19: 291–307, on which I have drawn extensively.

The phrase 'mental time travel' was coined by Tulving in his paper (1993) 'What is episodic memory?', *Current Directions in Psychological Science*, 2: 67–70.

Studies of the caching behaviour of scrub jays can be found in Clayton, N.S. and Dickinson, A. (1998) 'Episodic-like memory during cache recovery by scrub jays', *Nature*, 395: 272–8.

The claim that chimpanzees do not encourage their fellow chimpanzees to enter into their states of mind can be found in Tomasello, M. and Rakoczy, H. (2003) 'What makes human cognition unique? From individual to shared to collective intentionality', *Mind and Language*, 18: 121–47.

Details of the research indicating that debate and dissent foster thinking can be found in Nemeth, C.J. and Goncalo, J.A. (2011) 'Rogues and heroes: Finding value in dissent', in J. Jetten and M. Hornsey (eds) *Rebels in Groups: Dissent, Deviance, Difference and Defiance* (Wiley-Blackwell).

Kant's comment about examples functioning as the *gängelwagen* of thought is to be found in his *Critique of Pure Reason* (A 134, B 173–4).

Chapter 5: 'They don't think like we do'

The Levinson quotation, together with discussion of the studies mentioned, can be found in his book *Space in Language and Cognition: Explorations in Cognitive Diversity* (Cambridge, Cambridge University Press, 2003).

The study by Li and Papafragou on spatial reasoning in Tzeltal speakers can be found in P. Li et al. (2011) 'Spatial reasoning in Tenejapan Mayans', *Cognition*, 120: 33–53.

The claim that Micronesian Ifaluk believe that missing one's relatives might cause those relatives to become ill is reported in C. Lutz

(1985) 'Ethnopsychology compared to what? Explaining behaviour and consciousness among the Ifaluk', in G. White and J. Kirkpatrick (eds) *Person, Self and Experience* (Berkeley, University of California Press), pp. 35–79.

For cross-cultural research into the age at which children acquire an understanding of the mind see T. Callaghan et al. (2005) 'Synchrony in the onset of mental-state reasoning—Evidence from five cultures', *Psychological Science*, 16(5): 378–84.

Luria's studies on reasoning in Uzbekistan can be found in A.R. Luria, *Cognitive Development: Its Cultural and Social Foundations* (Cambridge, MA: Harvard University Press, 1976).

Information about the studies examining the differences between Americans and East Asians in modes of inference can be found in the following papers: Masuda, T. and R. Nisbett (2001) 'Attending holistically vs. analytically: Comparing the context sensitivity of Japanese and Americans,' *Journal of Personality and Social Psychology*, 81: 922–34; Ji, L-J., Zhang, Z. Nisbett, R. E. (2004) 'Is it culture or is it language? Examination of language effects in cross-cultural research on categorization,' *Journal of Personality and Social Psychology*, 87(1): 57–65; and A. Norenzayan et al. (2002) 'Cultural preferences for formal versus intuitive reasoning', *Cognitive Science*, 26: 653–84.

Whorf's writings on the linguistic determination of thought can be found in his *Language, Thought and Reality*, J.B. Carroll (ed.) (Cambridge, MA: MIT Press, 1956).

The study contrasting perception of blue in English speakers with that of Russian speakers can be found in J. Winawer et al. (2007) 'Russian blues reveal effects of language on color discrimination,' *Proceedings of the National Academy of Sciences* (USA), 104(19): 7780–85.

The study of the representation of stereotypes in Chinese–English bilinguals can be found in C. Hoffman et al. (1986) 'The linguistic relativity of person cognition: An English–Chinese comparison', *Journal of Personality and Social Psychology*, 51: 1097–1105.

The study of counting in English and Chinese can be found in Miller, K.F. and Stigler, J. (1987) 'Counting in Chinese: Cultural variation in a basic cognitive skill', *Cognitive Development*,' 2: 279–305.

The study of mathematical reasoning in Welsh and English bilingual children can be found in Ellis, N.C. and Hennelly, R.A. (1980) 'A bilingual word-length effect: Implications for intelligence testing and the relative ease of mental calculation in Welsh and English', *British Journal of Psychology*, 71: 43–51.

Information about mathematical cognition in the Pirahã and Mundurukú can be found in the following papers: M.C. Frank et al. (2008) 'Number as a cognitive technology: Evidence from Pirahã language and cognition', *Cognition*, 108: 819–24 and P. Pica et al. (2004) 'Exact and approximate arithmetic in an Amazonian indigene group', *Science*, 306: 499–503.

Chapter 6: Thought gone wrong

The case of the person who believed that her mother changed into another person every time she put her glasses on can be found in De Pauw, K.W. and Szulecka, T.K. (1988) 'Dangerous delusions: Violence and the Misidentification Syndromes', *British Journal of Psychiatry*, 152: 91–6.

The case of the man who claimed to have two heads is described in D. Ames (1984) 'Self shooting of a phantom head', *British Journal of Psychiatry*, 145: 193–4.

Details of Bentall's model of persecutory delusions can be found in his paper (1994) 'Cognitive biases and abnormal beliefs: Towards a model of persecutory delusions', in A.S. David and J.C. Cutting (eds) *The Neuropsychology of Schizophrenia* (Hove, E. Sussex: Psychology Press, 1994).

A seminal presentation of Maher's approach to delusions can be found in Maher, B.A. (1974) 'Delusional thinking and perceptual disorder', *Journal of Individual Psychology*, 30: 98–113.

For Ellis and Young's account of the Capgras delusion see Ellis, H.D. and Young, A.W. (1990) 'Accounting for delusional misidentifications', *British Journal of Psychiatry*, 157: 239–48.

Frith's model of delusions of alien control is developed in various places, including C. Frith et al. (2000) 'Explaining the symptoms of schizophrenia: Abnormalities in the awareness of action', *Brain Research Reviews*, 31: 357–63.

The finding that patients with delusions of alien control are able to tickle themselves is reported in S.-J. Blakemore et al. (2000) 'Why can't we tickle ourselves?', *NeuroReport*, 11: 11–16.

Stone and Young's proposed second factor for delusions can be found in Stone, T. and Young, A. (1997) 'Delusions and brain injury: The philosophy and psychology of belief', *Mind and Language*, 12: 327–64.

The data about a jumping-to-conclusions bias in belief-formation can be found in Garety, P.A. et al. (1999) 'Cognitive approaches to delusions: A critical review of theories and evidence', *British Journal of Clinical Psychology*, 38: 113–54.

Chapter 7: The ethics of thought

A review of Jonathan Schooler's work on mind wandering can be found in his paper (2002) 'Re-representing consciousness: dissociations between experience and meta-consciousness', *Trends in Cognitive Sciences*, 6/8, 339–44.

Daniel Wegner's work on the ironic control of thought can be found in his wonderfully entertaining book *White Bears and Other Unwanted Thoughts* (Guildford, 1994).

Peter van Inwagen's discussion of Clifford's dictum can be found in his paper (1998) 'It is wrong, everywhere, always, and for anyone, to believe anything upon insufficient evidence', which can be found in his book *The Possibility of Resurrection and Other Essays in Christian Apologetics* (Boulder, CO: Westview Press, 1997), on which my treatment of Clifford draws heavily.

Chapter 8: The limits of thought

The quotation from John Tyndall is drawn from his *Fragments of Science*, first published in 1871.

Colin McGinn's argument for mysterianism can be found in his book *The Mysterious Flame* (Cambridge MA: MIT Press, 1999).

Rae Langton's defence of Kantian Humility can be found in her book *Kantian Humility: Our Ignorance of Things in Themselves* (Oxford: Clarendon Press, 1998).

The quotation from Kant is taken from his *Critique of Pure Reason* (A51/B75).

The quotation from Rudolf Otto is to be found in his book *The Idea of the Holy* (New York: Oxford University Press, 1917/1958), p. 33.

The quotation from Pascal with which the chapter concludes is from his *Pensées* (§347).

Further reading

Chapter 1: What is thought?

Useful introductions to the intentional structure of thought can be found in John Searle's *Intentionality* and Tim Crane's *The Elements of Mind*. A collection of recent papers on the conscious character of thought can be found in *Cognitive Phenomenology* (Oxford: Oxford University Press, 2011), edited by Tim Bayne and Michelle Montague. Thomas Gilovich's *How We Know What Isn't So* (Free Press, 1993) contains many other examples of cognitive biases and is a great read. The 'bounded rationality' approach to reasoning has been developed in important ways by Gerd Gigerenzer and Daniel Goldstein in connection with the idea that much of human reasoning involves fast and frugal heuristics. See G. Gigerenzer and D. Goldstein (1996) 'Reasoning the fast and frugal way: Models of bounded rationality', *Psychological Review*, 103: 650–69. Daniel Kahnemann's *Thinking Fast and Slow* (Farrar, Straus and Giroux, 2011) provides a magisterial treatment of the relationship between intuitive (fast) and reflective (slow) thinking. The relevance of our cognitive limitations for an account of the norms of thought is a theme of Christopher Cherniak's book *Minimal Rationality* (Cambridge, MA: MIT, 1990).

Chapter 2: The mechanical mind

One of the best introductions to the computational theory of the mind is Tim Crane's *The Mechanical Mind* (London: Routledge, 2003), from which the title of this chapter takes its name. The most accessible version of Fodor's defence of the language of thought is to be found in

his book *Psychosemantics* (Cambridge, MA: MIT Press, 1987),
especially its first chapter. A collection of papers on the Chinese room
argument can be found in J. Preston and M. Bishop (eds) *Views into
the Chinese Room: New Essays on Searle and Artificial Intelligence*
(New York: Oxford University Press, 2002). Jack Copeland's *Artificial
Intelligence: A Philosophical Introduction* (Blackwell, Oxford, 1993) is
one of the best introductions to the philosophical issues raised by the
questions concerning the possibility of artificial thought. Robert
Cummins's *Meaning and Mental Representation* (Cambridge, MA:
MIT, 1989) provides a good (although not always easy) place to begin
for readers interested in the problems associated with explaining
mental content. Some of Dennett's worries about the computational
theory of thought can be found in his paper 'A cure for the common
code', in his *Brainstorms: Philosophical Essays on Mind and
Psychology* (Cambridge, MA: MIT Press, 1978). Discussion of the
dynamical challenge to the computational theory of mind can be
found in the following two papers by Tim van Gelder (1998) 'The
dynamical hypothesis in cognitive science', *Behavioral and Brain
Sciences*, 21(5): 615–28; and (1995) 'What might cognition be if not
computation?', *Journal of Philosophy*, 92: 345–81.

Chapter 3: The inner sanctum

A famous attack on the Cartesian conception of thought can be found
in Gilbert Ryle's *The Concept of Mind*. A more recent attack on the
Cartesian approach to self-knowledge, and one that draws on a great
deal of work in cognitive science, is Peter Carruthers's *The Opacity of
Mind* (New York: Oxford University Press, 2011). For an account of
first-person access to thought that is rather more sympathetic to the
Cartesian approach see Brie Gertler's *Self-Knowledge* (London:
Routledge, 2010). Good reviews of what we know about the
psychological processes implicated in mind-reading can be found in
Ian Apperly's *Mindreaders: The Cognitive Basis of Theory of Mind*
(Psychology Press, 2010) and Alvin Goldman's *Simulating Minds: The
Philosophy, Psychology and Neuroscience of Mindreading* (New York:
Oxford University Press, 2006). An engaging discussion of the
philosophical issues raised by brain-decoding can be found in Daniel
Dennett's paper 'Brain writing and mind reading', which is reprinted
in his book *Brainstorms* (Cambridge, MA: MIT Press, 1978). A more
recent examination of brain-decoding research and its implications for
our understanding of the mind can be found in *I Know What you are*

118

Thinking: Brain Imaging and Mental Privacy, edited by Sarah
Edwards, Sarah Richmond, and Geraint Rees (Oxford: Oxford
University Press, 2012).

Chapter 4: Brute thought

Two excellent collections of essays on animal thought are *Rational
Animals*? (Oxford: Oxford University Press, 2006), edited by Susan
Hurley and Matthew Nudds, and *The Philosophy of Animal Minds*,
edited by Robert Lutz (New York: Cambridge University Press, 2009).
The latter volume contains a particularly good chapter on social
thought in baboons by Elisabeth Camp. José Luis Bermúdez's *Thinking
Without Words* (New York: Oxford University Press, 2003) provides a
comprehensive study of the capacities of thought in non-linguistic
creatures. A critical analysis of the literature on metacognition in
animals can be found in Peter Carruthers's paper (2008) 'Metacognition in animals: A sceptical look', *Mind and Language*, 23: 58–89.
The idea that inner speech involves the internalization of external
processes can be found in the work of the Russian psychologist Lev
Vygotsky, in particular his book *Thought and Language* (Cambridge,
MA: MIT Press, 1986). The importance of the external environment in
facilitating thought has been emphasized by many of the authors
working in the field of situated cognition. See, for example, Edwin
Hutchins's *Cognition in the Wild* (Cambridge, MA: MIT Press, 2003)
and Andy Clark's *Natural-Born Cyborgs* (New York: Oxford University
Press, 2003). Further discussion of the factors that contribute to the
uniqueness of human thought can be found in the following works: M.
Tomasello and H. Rakoczy (2003) 'What makes human cognition
unique? From individual to shared to collective intentionality', *Mind
and Language*, 18: 121–47; T. Suddendorf and M. Corballis (2007) 'The
evolution of foresight: What is mental time travel and is it uniquely
human?', *Behavioral and Brain Sciences*, 30: 299–313; and Kim
Sterlney *Thought in a Hostile World* (Oxford: Blackwell, 2003).

Chapter 5: 'They don't think like we do'

G.E.R. Lloyd's wonderful book *Cognitive Variations: Reflections on the
Unity and Diversity of the Human Mind* (Oxford: Oxford University
Press, 2007) examines many of the themes mentioned in this chapter.
An important discussion of the heavy 'Western' bias in psychology can
be found in J. Henrich et al. (2010) 'The weirdest people in the

world?', *Behavioural and Brain Sciences*, 33, 2/3: 1–75. Cross-cultural differences in conceptions of the mind are charted in A. Lilliard (1998) 'Ethnopsychologies: cultural variations in theories of mind', *Psychological Bulletin*, 123/1: 3–32. An eminently readable summary of Richard Nisbett's influential work on the contrast between 'Western' and 'Asian' modes of thought can be found in his book *The Geography of Thought* (New York: Simon & Schuster, 2003). For a critical evaluation of the claims made by Nisbett and his colleagues see H. Mercier (2011) 'On the universality of argumentative reasoning', *Journal of Cognition and Culture*, 11: 85–113. Good reviews of the relationship between thought and language can be found in P. Bloom and F. Keil's paper (2001) 'Thinking through language', *Mind and Language*, 16/4: 351–67 and L. Gleitman and A. Papafragou (2005) 'Language and thought', in R. Morrison and K. Holyoak (eds) *The Cambridge Handbook of Thinking and Reasoning* (New York: Cambridge University Press, 2005).

Chapter 6: Thought gone wrong

Readers wishing to follow up the issues raised in this chapter might consult Jennifer Radden's *On Delusion* (Routledge, 2010) and Dominic Murphy's *Psychiatry in the Scientific Image* (Cambridge, MA: MIT Press, 2006). For an excellent discussion of delusions that integrates clinical case studies with cognitive neuroscience see P. W. Halligan and J. C. Marshall (eds) *Method in Madness: Case Studies in Cognitive Neuropsychiatry* (Hove: Psychology Press, 1996). A very different perspective on delusions is provided by Louis Sass's *The Paradoxes of Delusion: Wittgenstein, Schreber, and the Schizophrenic Mind* (Ithaca, NY: Cornell University Press, 1994), which contains a fascinating account of the florid delusions of the 19th-century German judge Daniel Paul Schreber. Readers wishing to delve further into the question of whether delusions are genuine beliefs should consult Lisa Bortolotti's *Delusions and Other Irrational Beliefs* (Oxford: Oxford University Press, 2009). An accessible overview of the currently influential 'two-factor' approach to monothematic delusions can be found in M. Coltheart et al. (2011) 'Delusional belief', *Annual Review of Psychology*, 62: 271–98.

Chapter 7: The ethics of thought

Bernard Williams's paper 'Deciding to Believe', published in his book *Problems of the Self* (New York: Cambridge, 1973), provides an excellent starting point for further reading on doxastic voluntarism. A number of the papers in *Knowledge, Truth, and Duty: Essays on Epistemic Justification, Responsibility, and Virtue*, edited by Matthias Steup (New York: Oxford University Press, 2001), also engage with the topics covered in this chapter. Additional discussion of the ethics of belief can be found in P. Hieronymi (2008) 'Responsibility for believing', *Synthese* 161, 357–373; S. Keller (2004). 'Friendship and belief' *Philosophical Papers*, 33: 329–351; and S. Stroud (2006) 'Epistemic partiality in friendship', *Ethics*, 116: 498–524. For an interesting defence of the claim that human beings are 'biologically engineered' to form a variety of misbeliefs see Ryan McKay and Daniel Dennett's (2009) 'The evolution of misbelief', *Behavioral and Brain Sciences*, 32(6): 493–510.

Chapter 8: The limits of thought

Further reading on the challenges posed by understanding consciousness can be found in David Chalmers' *The Conscious Mind* (New York: Oxford University Press, 1996) and Joseph Levine's *Purple Haze: The Puzzle of Consciousness* (New York: Oxford University Press, 2004). The philosopher Robert van Gulick provides a critical discussion of Mysterianism in his 'Are we just all armadillos anyway?', which can be found in N. Block et al. (eds). *The Nature of Consciousness* (Cambridge, MA: MIT Press, 1997). Further discussion of whether the nature of things in themselves might be beyond our ken can be found in David Lewis's 'Ramseyan Humility', in D. Braddon-Mitchell and R. Nola (eds) *Conceptual Analysis* and *Philosophical Naturalism* (Cambridge, MA: MIT Press, 2009) and R. Langton and C. Robichaud, 'Ghosts in the world machine? Humility and its alternatives', in A. Hazlett (ed) *New Waves in Metaphysics* (New York: Palgrave Macmillan, 2010). Expositions of the *via negativa* can be found in each of the world's major religions. In Hinduism the view can be found in the writings of Shankara; in Judaism it can be found in the work of Moses Maimonides; in Christianity it is closely associated with the writing of Meister Eckhard and Julian of Norwich; and in Islam it can be found in the writings of Al Ghazali and Ibn Miskawayh. A classic discussion of ineffability can be found in the book *Time and Eternity* (Princeton, NJ: Princeton University Press, 1952), by W.T. Stace. My own discussion of the *via negativa* is indebted to William P. Alston's paper (1956) 'Ineffability', *The Philosophical Review*, 65/4: 506–22.

Index

Thought

Thought

INTELLIGENCE
A Very Short Introduction
Ian J. Deary

People value their powers of thinking and most of us are interested in why some people seem to drive a highly tuned Rolls Royce brain while others potter along with a merely serviceable Ford Fiesta. This Very Short Introduction describes what psychologists have discovered about how and why people differ in their thinking powers.

The book takes readers from no knowledge about the science of human intelligence to a stage where they are able to make judgements for themselves about some of the key questions about human mental ability differences. Each chapter deals with a central issue that is both scientifically lively and of considerable general interest, and is structured around a diagram which is explained in the course of the chapter. The issues discussed include whether there are several different types of intelligence, whether intelligence differences are caused by genes or the environment, the biological basis of intelligence differences, and whether intelligence declines or increases as we grow older.

www.oup.com/vsi

THE MEANING OF LIFE
A Very Short Introduction
Terry Eagleton

'Philosophers have an infuriating habit of analysing questions rather than answering them', writes Terry Eagleton, who, in these pages, asks the most important question any of us ever ask, and attempts to answer it. So what is the meaning of life? In this witty, spirited, and stimulating inquiry, Eagleton shows how centuries of thinkers - from Shakespeare and Schopenhauer to Marx, Sartre and Beckett - have tackled the question. Refusing to settle for the bland and boring, Eagleton reveals with a mixture of humour and intellectual rigour how the question has become particularly problematic in modern times. Instead of addressing it head-on, we take refuge from the feelings of 'meaninglessness' in our lives by filling them with a multitude of different things: from football and sex, to New Age religions and fundamentalism.

'Light hearted but never flippant.'

The Guardian.